ETHICAL QUESTIONS IN HEALTHCARE CHAPLAINCY

of related interest

Chaplaincy in Hospice and Palliative Care
Edited by Karen Murphy and Bob Whorton
Foreword by Baroness Finlay of Llandaff
ISBN: 978 1 78592 068 4
eISBN: 978 1 78450 329 1

Critical Care
Delivering Spiritual Care in Healthcare Contexts
Edited by Jonathan Pye, Peter Sedgwick and Andrew Todd
ISBN: 978 1 84905 497 3
eISBN: 978 0 85700 901 2

Spiritual Care in Practice
Case Studies in Healthcare Chaplaincy
Edited by George Fitchett and Steve Nolan
ISBN: 978 1 84905 976 3
eISBN: 978 0 85700 876 3

ETHICAL QUESTIONS IN HEALTHCARE CHAPLAINCY

LEARNING TO MAKE INFORMED DECISIONS

Pia Matthews

Jessica Kingsley *Publishers*
London and Philadelphia

First published in 2018
by Jessica Kingsley Publishers
73 Collier Street
London N1 9BE, UK
and
400 Market Street, Suite 400
Philadelphia, PA 19106, USA

www.jkp.com

Library of Congress Cataloging in Publication Data
Names: Matthews, Pia, author.
Title: Ethical questions in healthcare chaplaincy / Pia Matthews.
Description: Philadelphia : Jessica Kingsley Publishers, 2018.
Identifiers: LCCN 2018000276 | ISBN 9781785924217
Subjects: LCSH: Medical ethics--Religious aspects. | Chaplains, Hospital.
Classification: LCC R725.55 .M38 2018 | DDC 174.2--dc23 LC record available at
https://lccn.loc.gov/2018000276

British Library Cataloguing in Publication Data
A CIP catalogue record for this book is available from the British Library

ISBN 978 1 78592 421 7
eISBN 978 1 78450 788 6

Printed and bound in Great Britain

CONTENTS

INTRODUCTION

Consider this all too common situation for healthcare chaplains:

> *The chaplain has been called to the maternity ward. In a side room, he finds Amy obviously devastated, sitting in silence next to her husband Ben, who is gently stroking his wife's hand. Claire, the nurse, stands near a baby's cot that is completely covered by a pink blanket.*

What should you do?

The 'what should you do?' is an ethical question. What you do next and how you do it may make all the difference to the people in this situation. In this intense and emotionally charged situation there is no 'one size fits all' answer and the chaplain must make a quick decision on how best to respond.

> *After sitting with Amy and Ben for a while in silence, the chaplain eventually learns that the couple had had IVF (in vitro fertilization), so that they could have this much-longed-for child who is now dead. 'Is God punishing us?' asks Amy. The chaplain also discovers that the parents have not seen or held their baby yet.*

In times of intensity we are often tempted to act immediately and intuitively. We think we know what is best, even before we have all the relevant facts. Without further conversation with the couple, and especially without active listening, the chaplain may make assumptions about Amy's fears. The chaplain may also make decisions that are too quick about what to say and what is to be done.

Ben asks the chaplain to baptise their baby.

When chaplains are asked to do something specific, they must think carefully about the situation. Chaplains have to deal not only with the ethics and the moral sensibilities of the people involved but also with their own ethical and theological framework. In particular, chaplains must be mindful of their loyalty to their own faith tradition, since they are, after all, representatives of that tradition.

The chaplain goes over to the cot and finds the nurse, Claire, who also seems to be upset.

Although a chaplain is usually called to minister to a particular patient, there are often more people involved who also require spiritual support. This includes not only family, carers and close friends of the patient but also healthcare colleagues.

Claire whispers that Amy had a termination, because the baby was diagnosed with a disability. Claire tells the chaplain that she feels upset and does not know what to do. She says that she was not sure that Amy and Ben could make an informed decision to terminate the pregnancy. The couple were so devastated by the news that their baby might be disabled that they could not 'think straight'. She says that the doctor told Amy and Ben that their baby would not be born alive as a result of the termination procedure. But Claire thinks that Amy and Ben did not realise that part of the process involved stopping the baby's heart before it was born. Claire knows that Amy and Ben did not expect their baby to be born alive, but she does not think they are aware of the full reality of the situation. Claire is worried in case Amy and Ben ask her any specific questions, and she asks the chaplain if she should tell them the truth.

> **REFLECTION**
>
> In complex situations, do you look for what is good or what is right, or what makes people happy or what works? What do you need to help you respond ethically?

About this book

Ethical Questions in Healthcare Chaplaincy cannot tell you how to respond to each and every situation. However, a study of ethics does help to clarify issues, to separate out important factors, to prioritise and to identify our duties and our values, so that we can move forward and help others also to move on and adjust to a new reality. A study of ethics helps to appreciate differing viewpoints and develop an ethical and critically reflective approach to difficult questions.

This book is written for healthcare chaplains and from the perspective of healthcare chaplaincy. This is not to say that ethical inquiry for healthcare chaplains is separate from or even radically different to ethical inquiry for other healthcare practitioners or those in other fields. There is much in this book that is of relevance, and I hope of interest, to other people – after all, healthcare and spirituality are the concerns of everyone. Nevertheless, this book aims to help healthcare chaplains reflect on and learn to respond to the particular ethical demands made on them in their particular context. The healthcare chaplain's context is built up of a complex network of ethical relationships. Not only does the chaplain have to think and act ethically, the chaplain must also support others to make their own ethical decisions. Moreover, people supported by the chaplain come with their own complex sets of needs and difficulties that may be medical, psychological, ethical and spiritual. These needs and difficulties may affect their decision-making.

However, the support offered by chaplains is not simply around decision-making; it is also around how to manage spiritual and existential crises. In ministering to individuals, families, carers, friends and other healthcare colleagues, the chaplain's role has been neatly though perhaps inadequately described as to *pacify, clarify, satisfy*: the chaplain calms the person down, identifies the central issues and then helps the person work out what is needed. We can think of this using the analogy of a fly in a bottle which is constantly banging into the transparent glass sides in an effort to escape. The chaplain is there to coax the fly to find its own way out of the top of the bottle. In human terms, this pacify, clarify, satisfy aspect of the chaplain's role can only be successful if there is trust between the chaplain and the people involved.

Trust is a good reason why one of the essential capabilities for healthcare chaplaincy is practising ethically. At a minimum, practising ethically involves recognising the rights of patients, families and carers; providing information in order to improve understanding, to help to inform choice and to support decision-making. Practising ethically also includes providing care that is based on professional, legal and ethical codes of practice. However, all of the essential capabilities for healthcare chaplaincy have an ethical dimension – working in partnership with individuals, families and colleagues is a mark of respect for the ethical relationship in which the chaplain works. Respecting diversity, identifying people's needs, providing safe and responsive patient care and recognising the relevance of rehabilitation and self-care are all illustrations of the ethical demands of respecting the dignity of every person; challenging inequality is an ethical demand of justice. Promoting good practice and pursuing personal development are examples of the ethical call for critical self-reflection, examination of good and less good practice and striving to do better.

Much good practice in healthcare is already built into the practice of medicine itself. Good practice such as safeguarding, seeking consent and respecting confidentiality arises from the fact that human beings have dignity and rights that must be respected. This respect is reflected in ethical codes of practice and conduct as well as in legislation. Certainly, chaplains must be aware of these codes and relevant legislation, so that they can give wise guidance and support. However, sometimes principles seem to conflict.

There are several possible courses of action, and when faced with the same set of facts different people arrive at different solutions. Moreover, at times of crisis, people may be paralysed in their thinking, or they may rely on an immediate intuitive judgement and action. As part of good practice, the chaplain should develop a reflective approach to ethical questions. This involves critical and evaluative reasoning that is also sensitive to the complex needs of the people to whom the chaplain ministers. Moreover, the chaplain should take a theological approach to ethics. Taking a theological approach is a reminder that the vocation of the healthcare chaplain has both a horizontal dimension that reaches out to relationships with the people involved, and also a vertical dimension that reaches to a relationship with God.

In this book, we use a case-study approach. These case studies are entirely fictitious and they usually contain more ethical issues than would be found in one particular situation. The case studies are not there to suggest that a patient may have been treated in an unprincipled or uncared-for way. After all, most people who work in healthcare seek to act ethically and with integrity. The case studies do, however, indicate that sometimes pressures highlight gaps or unreflective thinking in care. The case studies are there to prompt your reflection as a chaplain on how to support people spiritually, pastorally and ethically, on potential mistakes or gaps in action and inaction and on some of the profound truths of healthcare.

In order to work through ethical thinking, it is important to pay attention to core values that are imbedded in healthcare and to relevant legislation and procedures. However, there are different approaches to difficult questions. This is why we also have to look at different ethical frameworks.

Information: core values, legislation and ethical frameworks

Learning how to respond to ethical questions in healthcare chaplaincy concerns action as well as attitudes. Ethics is not simply about what the chaplain does. It is also, and perhaps more significantly, about what kind of person the chaplain is. The chaplain is engaged in work that requires among other things a sense of identity as well as sensitivity, discernment, an understanding of power imbalances, appreciating boundaries, being mindful of both the horizontal and vertical dimensions of chaplaincy. This means that any account of ethics demands attention not only to the question in hand and ethical approaches to that question, but also to dispositions of character or virtues – and dispositions of character are very much involved in our practical behaviour. This is why *Ethical Questions in Healthcare Chaplaincy* asks you, the reader, to reflect on your action, on what informs your thinking and practice, and on how you are challenged by what you read.

As almost every code of practice, guideline and healthcare standard recognises, the only appropriate relationship between chaplains and those in their care is 'a professional relationship committed to promote the spiritual good and best interests of particular individuals'.[1] Inevitably, the chaplain is engaged in ethical relationships, relationships which are basic and trustworthy, where what we do and what we fail to do has an impact in that sacred space between chaplains and those they serve.

We can identify a set of minimum core values and 'asks' in the ethical relationship between chaplains and those in their care, and these 'asks' say something about the character dispositions expected of healthcare chaplains. *Safeguarding* asks us to protect people's health, wellbeing and rights, so that they live free from harm, abuse and neglect. *Personal responsibility* asks us to take charge of what we do and what we fail to do, and it requires us to build up and strengthen that sacred space of the ethical relationship. *Personal accountability* asks us to be honest, open and able to justify our practice, and it calls for

---

1   UK Board of Healthcare Chaplaincy (2010, revised 2014) *Code of Conduct for Healthcare Chaplains*, 4, p.8

transparency in the way in which we deal with others. *Respect* asks us actively to recognise the dignity of all those we encounter, and it demands that we promote and communicate respect for the dignity of every person regardless of age, culture, religion, state of life or situation. *Care* asks us to be care-ful by listening to and taking account of the concerns of others, and it advances true compassion that avoids both callousness and pity. *Integrity* asks us to be sincere, reliable and consistent, and it expects us to maintain knowledge, skills and capabilities so that we can practise safely, ethically, competently and legally.

Although we may be able to identify some core values – and you may wish to add to these yourself – there is also *legislation* such as the Mental Capacity Act 2005 and the Data Protection Act 1998, and there are *codes of practice* and *standards* as well as the specific procedures of your institution that come with the job. Of course, guidelines are carefully researched and written by experts to enable healthcare professionals and patients to make the best decisions in particular situations, and professionals are encouraged to follow the guidelines where appropriate. However, some situations do not fit neatly into the guidelines and some guidelines are controversial. Simply following a guideline does not absolve a person from using their own judgement. Moreover, the chaplain must be aware that there may be occasions when a guideline seems to conflict with conscience or faith.

While some people do just *follow the guidelines* or do what they perceive is their *duty*, other people may point to patient *rights*, *autonomy* and *choice* as the only thing relevant in ethics. Giving such priority to patient autonomy is to forget that we are not isolated individuals, that what we do has implications for others and indeed the autonomy of others. The other side of the coin to autonomy is *paternalism*, where the doctor decides, acting in what he or she sees as the best interests of the patient, but this may take no account of the patient's wishes, values or beliefs. Some people may think that the *consequences* of the action are the only things that matter.

Others follow *utilitarianism* by balancing what they see as goods such as amounts of pleasure or happiness against evils such as pain or unhappiness in order to calculate an overall result where goods outweigh evils. However, happiness is notoriously difficult to define. We cannot foresee all possible consequences and many aspects of healthcare are not ready subjects of a mechanical calculation. Moreover, acting solely on the possibility of achieving good consequences would allow a person to do acts that many people see as morally wrong.

Another approach often used in healthcare is the *principles* approach. Following this approach, we can analyse ethical problems by using a framework of four principles: respect for autonomy that enables choice; non-maleficence that is an obligation not to inflict harm intentionally; beneficence that refers to actions done for the benefit of others; justice that treats equals equally. The problem here is that sometimes there will be conflicts between the principles and often the decision-maker has already decided which principle to apply before determining which may be more appropriate.

It may seem that this list of different ethical approaches serves only to complicate issues. Nevertheless, the purpose of showing that there is a plurality of approaches should alert each one of us to the fact that people do have different ethical frameworks, and, if we can recognise this, then we can discuss ethics with them in a respectful manner. Identifying our own framework and that of the other person enables us to reflect together.

Aside from these different approaches, often how we decide what to do varies. Sometimes we simply act out of habit and do what we have always done without really thinking. Sometimes we just do what everyone else is doing. However, in the sacred space of the ethical relationship between healthcare chaplains and those for whom we care, the practice of ethics is not like a hobby which we can take up or discontinue as we feel. Nor is the practice of ethics purely a private matter for the individual based on their feelings about the issue. An ethical approach based solely on feelings that says, 'I feel it is right, therefore it is right' is a shaky grounding for professional ethics. If moral opinions are based on my feelings and nothing more then, since I cannot be wrong in how I feel, there is no real check on my action. I can justify anything I do by my feelings, even if you think my action is wrong. Rather than appeal to feelings, we may want to appeal to reason. If I use reason, then it seems that I will act consistently in the same way to everyone. This is not to say that emotions and feelings have no part in ethical decision-making. Feelings encourage empathy, moral imagination, putting myself in the other person's shoes, and they often lie behind the choices I make and the reasons I give. Reason checks my feelings, it helps me act justly and to put into action what I think should be done. Feelings and reason governed by virtuous character dispositions enable me to exercise practical wisdom and act well even in difficulties, in a balanced way, with proper concern for others.

So, reason, feelings, empathy, character, practical wisdom and an eye to the situation all are factors in our responses to ethical questions. But where does religion fit in? For some people, religion is an additional factor – we can understand the situation and work out what to do, and our religious traditions or beliefs give a further reason for acting in a particular way. For other people, religion is a motivating force – because we hold certain beliefs we are encouraged to act in a particular way. For others, the very fact that we hold to a faith tradition means that we see situations and issues in the light of that tradition – religion is neither added on nor simply motivating, rather it is like a torch that lights up issues, enabling us to act in a particular way.

We may wish to factor in here different understandings of conscience and how a person acts according to conscience. There will be more on conscience and conscientious objection later in Chapter 11. But for now, it is enough perhaps to say that in responding to ethical questions I should try always to do what is good. Sometimes I may get it wrong. In learning to respond I need to reflect, to discern, to listen to good advice, and to take notice of examples of good practice.

How to approach an ethical issue

Here are a few pointers that will help you get started: they are based on the idea that chaplains *see, judge, act*.

See by journeying together with the people you minister to in order to understand reality with the eyes of faith and heart of God.

- See what is happening by getting a simple grasp of the situation. This involves having a clear and basic description of what has happened and what is happening. The kinds of questions that may be useful here are: does this involve an ethical issue? Do you have enough information? Are you the person to deal with this? Who have you been called to support? What are the indicators of spiritual distress?

- Journey together. This involves taking things at a careful pace so that people can begin to understand what is happening. Some questions to ask yourself are: is this a time for just being there? What is the person feeling and saying? Is someone asking for something specific? How resilient is the person? Can you find empathy?

- Look at the reality of the situation. This involves breaking down the situation into parts. Questions to ask are: can you identify the relevant ethical aspects? Can you set aside the irrelevant aspects? Can you name what has happened and what causes concern? How are people dealing with this new reality?

Judge the situation not the people involved with theological reflection, and with mercy and compassion in the light of truth.

- Notice whether there is a significant aspect that requires special and perhaps immediate attention: is there, for instance, a clear case for safeguarding? Is this therefore your priority? How will this affect the people involved? Will it add to spiritual distress?

- Look at additional information: are there questions to do with confidentiality, consent or patient capacity? What about the dignity of the person?

- Check whether any legislation, professional guidance or procedures apply: do you know where to find the guidelines and protocols of your organisation? How do they fit with conscience in this particular situation?

Act from prayer, faith and hope by planning and carrying out what needs to be done.

- Critically analyse the situation: do you need to seek advice?

- Avoid imposing your own view: have you talked through how the person sees the situation? Have you identified what the person fears, values, prefers and hopes for?

- What else needs to be done to meet the spiritual needs of the person? Prayer and ritual?

The advantage of the *see, judge, act* model is that it encourages the chaplain to stop, to stand back from the situation, and to reflect. In this way, the chaplain is not tempted simply to jump in and act. Certainly at times the stages overlap. Nevertheless, the model does help to develop critical analysis and reflection on what are often complex situations.

The *see, judge, act* model gives space for prayer and discernment. It helps to identify and examine root causes of a problem and arrive at care-ful decisions. It allows us to consider whose voice needs to be heard and whose voice is missing. It calls on us to recognise the values and beliefs of the other people involved. It reminds us that there are struggles and cultural factors at play. It asks us to include wisdom and insights from our religious traditions. It enables us to judge the impact of our actions especially in terms of justice and what we hope for in a particular situation.

And thinking about the sacred space between the chaplain and the client

There is perhaps the art of *POETRY* in the way in which the healthcare chaplain creates that sacred space between the chaplain and the person:

Prayer is the foundation for all that the chaplain does.

Observation is vital to gauge the situation: observe hospital signs and notices, so that you are aware if the patient has low immunity, or if infection controls are in place or if the patient is 'nil by mouth'; observe the patient, so that you can work out if your visit is welcome, if they are too tired for a long visit, if they seem depressed or in pain; observe body language and non-verbal communication that may indicate the real message that the patient wishes to convey.

Engage with the person by making eye contact, by smiling, by adopting a friendly voice tone, by addressing the person by name.

Time is one of the most valued things you can give a person, and this includes letting the person set the agenda for the conversation, giving time for active listening without interruption, accepting silence and being with the person.

Remember the person not only the next time you meet or in follow-up activity or in the paperwork but also in your prayers.

Finally, **y**ou: there is an old saying that you cannot give what you do not have. This is why your own spirituality, your prayer life, self-care, and reflection on your practice are so important. Developing your own spiritual space where you can experience the very many inner voices of thoughts, emotions, feelings, passions without becoming overwhelmed or swept away, and then being open to emptying yourself, so that you can reflect what the person in conversation with you is expressing, is an important aspect of communication with the other.

Case study: ethical implications

See: Who have you been called to support: Amy and Ben certainly, but what about Claire? And respect for the baby even though her very short life is now over? Looking at the reality of the situation, what is your theological reflection on termination, on disability? How relevant is the fact that the baby was born through IVF? And the freedom of Amy and Ben? While they did make a decision, was their decision-making truly free or were they too overcome by their situation? Is belief in God's punishment the cause of spiritual distress?

Judge: What needs to be done? What are your priorities? Is encouraging Amy and Ben to hold their baby a way to healing? To what extent, if any, does this depend on the extent of the baby's disabilities? Is there a question about the professionalism of healthcare practitioners and providing patients with adequate information so that they can come to informed decisions? Do you have a concern about the doctor's approach? If so, do you know how to raise your concerns sensitively and productively?

Act: Blessing the baby? Arranging the funeral? What about the paperwork? And forgiveness?

Some further comments

Prayer is one of the greatest gifts that a chaplain can bring to a tragic and painful situation. A deep prayer life grounds the chaplain in all he does. Moreover, by asking Amy and Ben if they would like him to pray with them, the chaplain begins to open up a sacred space for their encounter. However, chaplains who do not share the same faith as those to whom they have been called must be aware of different faith sensibilities: a Christian chaplain who attends a Buddhist patient cannot pray *to* a Buddhist god; a Muslim chaplain attending a Christian patient cannot pray *to* Jesus as God. A chaplain can always pray *for* people.

Observe not only Amy and Ben but also Claire. Careful observation will ensure that the chaplain does not rush to conclusions or make quick assumptions. If the baby had significant disabilities, Amy and Ben may not wish to see her or may need considerable preparation first. If they are overwhelmed by a sense of loss, grief or even guilt and fear of punishment, now may not be the time.

Engaging with Amy and Ben involves attentive listening, hearing the whole of their difficult journey, letting them share their feelings and talking about the mercy of God. In this situation, the chaplain is not asked to be judgemental about such things as IVF, though of course the chaplain should be aware of the stand of his faith tradition on various medical technologies and procedures and should be prepared to explain should the couple ask. The chaplain should also be able to explain his response to specific requests. In this case, baptism in say the Catholic tradition would not be appropriate, since sacraments are for the living. Now that the baby is with God she does not need baptism. However, the chaplain can bless the baby and encourage the parents to give her a name. When they are ready, the chaplain can also talk about the funeral and what Amy and Ben might want.

Time is important here as this is not a situation that can be rushed. It may be more practical to deal with Claire's concerns at a later date.

Above all, the chaplain should remember to follow this up and to follow up the work with Amy and Ben. Eventually, an invitation to a service of remembrance may bring special healing. It goes without saying that being called to a baby who has died is not at all unusual.

You can easily become either hardened to this or overwhelmed by it, so remember to take care of yourself as well – and do the paperwork.

Outline of the chapters

This case-study approach to learning how to respond to ethical questions does not assume an in-depth knowledge of ethics. Some of the case studies represent day-to-day ethical issues encountered by healthcare chaplains. Some of the case studies present more challenging ethical problems. By including both apparently routine and more unusual scenarios we would like to demonstrate that ethics is not only about ethical dilemmas or conundrums, but neither is there an ethical dilemma under every hospital bed. After all, if a patient with a hearing aid does not appear to be engaging with a conversation about treatment such that the nurse begins to think the patient does not have capacity to make a decision, before reaching for the Mental Capacity Act assessment form, perhaps check that the patient's hearing aid has batteries and is switched on.

In each chapter, as ethical questions unfold, we are not presenting a puzzle which can be solved by working out all the clues to get to the right answer. However, this does not mean that there are no right answers or indeed no answers at all. If that were the case, we would be left with an endless debate. Instead we hope that you can relate to the different scenarios; that you can think of similar cases in your own experience; that you can reflect on what you read and can then generalise what you have learned.

In Chapter 1 we explore some of the basic dos and don'ts, and we draw a distinction between ethics and etiquette. A discussion of both etiquette and ethics will help us to realise that how we understand human dignity is a central concern in healthcare ethics, and so this is the focus of Chapter 2. In Chapter 3 we go deeper into questions of human dignity and explore ethical questions surrounding autonomy, consent and boundaries. You can find discussion of the Mental Capacity Act 2005 in this chapter and more explicitly in Chapter 4, where we look at patients who do not have autonomy. Once we have laid a foundation for the ethics regarding human dignity, then in Chapter 5 we build on these foundations by examining the principles of confidentiality, privacy, data protection, truth telling and trust that are foundational for healthcare chaplaincy practice. The Data Protection Act 1998 is particularly relevant here. Then as a kind of pairing, in Chapter 6 and Chapter 7, we think about the beginning of life and ethical issues relating to babies and young children, followed by, in Chapter 8 and Chapter 9, the end of life and issues relating to dying and death. Chapter 10 takes account of the ethics involved in grief and bereavement as well as self-care. Chapter 11 looks at conscience, conscientious objection and the loyalties that we hold, particularly where there is conflict.

You can find additional resources, guidelines and links to best practice in the Resources section at the end of this book.

> **REFLECTION**
>
> The last time you made a significant ethical decision in your role as a healthcare chaplain, what method did you use?

Summary

The case study at the beginning of this Introduction is representative of the kind of ethical situations in which chaplains find themselves. As you go through the book, you will be able to reflect critically on similar situations, and some of the other case studies will shed light on this first study.

Sometimes to speak just of ethics is inadequate, because the work of the chaplain is complex. The context for responding to ethical questions in healthcare embraces the chaplain's faith tradition, beliefs, values, spirituality, prayer life and how she sees the relationship between chaplain and client. You are asked to read with generosity and forgiveness: generosity for trying to encompass such an intricate subject; forgiveness for any difficulties that this causes you.

Chapter 1

THE BASICS

CASE STUDY

I began my day with morning prayer, on my own. It helps me to focus for the day ahead. Luckily, last evening I was not called out, so I could work on the memorial service we as a team are planning for miscarriages, stillborn babies and babies who have died. At Reception, I spend a few minutes with the hospital friend, one of those volunteers who help people find where they are going. She happens to be one of my parishioners with a heart of gold who loves to chat 'in confidence'. She always asks me how things are, how busy I am, who I am visiting, and what is new. Today she tells me that she has just seen one of our fellow parishioners being admitted to the hospital. She asks if the parishioner should be named on the parish prayer list and if I can let her know when I have visited.

When I get to the office, I check for any messages or referrals and I draw up my visiting list for the day. Usually I do this while chatting with the rest of the team – we are a multi-faith chaplaincy – and we also have to coordinate with the volunteers. On to the ward I dutifully wash my hands – there is a lot of handwashing. I speak to the senior nurse on duty, and then I introduce myself to a patient and his family who are waiting for test results. I promise I will come back to see how they got on. The patient in the next bed asks if I can help, even though I am a Christian chaplain. She is Jewish and wants someone to come for a chat. She also says that she is desperate for a drink of water. I get a call from Accident and Emergency (A&E). Fortunately, the new patient's condition is not life threatening, and I check if she wants her family to be called. Up on the geriatric ward, a patient has had complications after routine surgery. I talk to the daughter and suggest she calls in other members of the family, just in case. I lead a short prayer at her mother's bedside and we agree that a service of anointing would be in order. I understand from the nurse that the family may be asked to make a decision about withdrawing treatment. The nurse is a Catholic, and she is worried in case this means her patient will not continue to have food and fluids.

As I am leaving the ward, another nurse comes up to me and wants to complain about the ward sister. With so much going on I nearly forget that I have promised to go back to the patient waiting for his test results. Suddenly there is commotion on the ward as a rather confused elderly patient starts shouting. He has seen that I am a chaplain, and he is saying that he needs to confess. He shouts that he has been abusing young children for years and now he is so sorry. What a day! And I have still got the paperwork to do.

REFLECTION

As you read this fictional day in the life of a chaplain, which aspects coincide with your experiences? At any point did you notice any areas of real concern or difficulty? The case study does not tell you what the chaplain did in response to some of the situations. Which situation was the most challenging for you? What would you have done? Is handwashing an ethical issue?

Etiquette and ethics

We usually think of etiquette as good manners or polite behaviour. Professional etiquette is often regarded as the traditions of social behaviour that help the smooth running of the profession. With its focus on social behaviour, etiquette seems to be external. It reflects the professional's concern about how her behaviour is perceived by others. Alternatively, ethics seems to be internal because ethics involves intentions, decisions, justifications, and the apparently more important questions of how and why the person acts.

Certainly, etiquette can hide poor practice – I can be polite to the patient and at the same time fail out of negligence to respond to the patient's needs. However, etiquette can also be an external manifestation of sound moral character and intention. There are things that chaplains do and refrain from doing that seem to be merely what is expected of them. Simply out of politeness I may introduce myself to the patient so that the patient knows who I am.

In healthcare, professional etiquette is more than good manners. If we think of what we do as part of the way in which we establish relationships of respect with patients, families, carers and colleagues in what amounts to a sacred space then there is not such a great difference between ethics and etiquette, the internal and external aspects of the healthcare chaplain. The way we behave from how we present ourselves to what we actually do and say sets the tone, as it were, for our relationships with others. If we appear to be disorganised, rushed, unfriendly or over-friendly, even careless in our appearance, then this will affect the tone of the relationship we are establishing. Acting with courtesy, being caring and helpful, aids in establishing a positive relationship.

Information: dos and don'ts
Preparing to visit

- Follow procedures that are specific to your organisation; for example, if there is a sign-in system, make sure you sign in.

- Wear your hospital ID (means of identification).

- Follow the process for recording referrals and requests.

- Use the antiseptic hand gel on entering and leaving the ward and after visiting a patient.

- Note any signs indicating barrier nursing or infection control.

- Introduce yourself to the ward sister.

- Ask if there is anyone who would like a visit or anyone who should not be disturbed.

With the patient

- Pray.

- Remember you are entering the patient's world and the patient's protected space.

- Introduce yourself – this will confirm whether you are the person the patient has asked for.

- Ask permission – this allows the person to have some control over their personal space.

- Sit on a chair if the patient wants you to stay. This way you will not be looking down at the patient.

- Watch out for catheters or drains – often these are hidden under the blankets.

- Accept the patient as they are.

- Let the patient lead the conversation. The patient may not want to talk immediately about religion without finding out about you first.

- If you are a minister or priest but not a member of the hospital chaplaincy team, let the hospital chaplain know you have visited.

- Pray.

Don't

- Do not visit if you are unwell.

- Do not wake the patient up.

- Never fully draw the curtain or shut the door.

- Do not do things that the patient can do for themselves.

- Try not to argue with the patient.

- Refrain from criticising the patient's faith or beliefs or lifestyle.

- Do not attempt to diagnose their illness or compare it with your own health issues.

- Do not give the patient anything to eat or drink without checking with the nursing staff first.

- Do not lift the patient.

- Do not help the patient in or out of bed.

- Do not accept any money.

- Do not light candles, especially when there may be oxygen around, for instance in the intensive care unit.

Case study: ethical implications

See: With the pressures of a busy day, do you sometimes miss the realities of some situations? Being aware that an apparently routine situation has ethical implications requires skill and experience. Are you always aware of times when confidentiality is at risk of being broken? How hard is it to keep professional boundaries? If you are fortunate to work in a multi-faith team, do you call on your colleagues where appropriate? Is referring a patient of a particular faith to their own chaplain simply a matter of courtesy, or is it a matter of respect for the patient and for their faith tradition? Do you notice the pressures on other members of staff?

Judge: Safeguarding is a priority. Did you recognise this? Are you prepared to find out about relevant procedures or ask other colleagues, in particular the nursing staff, in situations where you are uncertain?

Act: In situations involving issues such as safeguarding there are clear procedures to follow – do you know what these are? Do you act on your concerns? Do you remember to make appropriate spiritual assessments for the patient and family members?

Some further comments

The first person that the chaplain meets is the hospital friend who likes to chat 'in confidence' in the hospital reception area. How will you deal with this? Of course, hospital friends are generally the most discrete and careful of people, who have undergone training for their position, but the point of including this as an ethical situation should be clear: people often are friendly, especially if you see them on a regular basis or have a connection with them outside of the hospital setting. It is important that you have good and appropriately friendly relationships with all those you meet. However, both in private and in public spaces, the chaplain must both *see* and *judge* whether there are significant issues of confidentiality and privacy. We shall discuss boundaries in Chapter 3, and the requirements of confidentiality in Chapter 4. Suffice it to say that no one outside the hospital has a right to know a person is a patient, and so adding someone to a church prayer list without their express permission breaches confidentiality. Although anyone – relatives, friends, hospital staff and members of the patient's faith community – can make a referral to the chaplaincy team, it is part of good hospital practice to *act*, so that all patients and service users are asked about their religion or beliefs on admission, are given a spiritual assessment if this is what they want, and are offered the appropriate chaplaincy support. Information can only be passed back to the person who referred the patient, if the patient expressly agrees. We shall explore issues of autonomy and consent in Chapter 3.

Hospital volunteers often play a vital if unacknowledged part in patient and family care. For volunteers, having a sense of belonging to a team and feeling valued is important, as it is for everyone. Certainly, you do not have to be 'on the job' all the time, but you need to *see* with broad vision and you may wish to consider what spiritual needs the hospital friend would like to share with you. You may also wish to remind the person gently and with sensitivity of the need for professionalism and confidentiality.

Working as a team ensures that spiritual care is delivered effectively and by the appropriate person. Who is in the chaplaincy team can vary from one hospital to another, and where there are complex ethical questions, it is important to *judge* and know the relevant lines of responsibility and authority. Moreover, having proper regard for the health and wellbeing of chaplains themselves is an aspect of good ethical practice. Usually there is a lead chaplain who manages and supervises the chaplaincy team and individual chaplains. There may even be a specialist chaplain with expertise in a particular area of medicine. Often there are volunteer visitors and chaplaincy support workers who work under the supervision of a chaplain. Volunteer chaplains and support workers support patients and visitors, but they refer more complex cases to their supervising chaplain. These volunteers may include people who are recognised by their particular faith community to provide pastoral care to a member of that community, and the names of these volunteers should be listed in the chaplaincy department. Chaplains are qualified practitioners with specific roles and responsibilities depending on their band. Practitioners, from volunteers to specialist and lead chaplains, work within the parameters of National Health Service (NHS) chaplaincy guidelines.

It is important for you as a chaplain to realise that you are not working in isolation: chaplains work with each other and with other healthcare practitioners. Chaplains are also there to support other healthcare staff. Requirements such as handwashing and wearing protective clothing apply as much to the chaplain as to any other healthcare professional. We will discuss the *act* of handwashing as an ethical issue at the end of this chapter.

As a matter of courtesy, you should make yourself known to the senior nurse on duty and to other healthcare colleagues. On a practical level this gives nurses the opportunity to let you know the ward routine, where a patient might be, and if there are any specific issues that you may encounter, from infection control to patient needs. It also recognises the authority and responsibility of the senior nurse. On a spiritual level, nurses have needs as well and they are often subject to criticism and negativity as well as praise. However, you have come to see a specific patient: can you apply *POETRY* here, even if only in part? Does it help?

The chaplain is said to 'loiter with intent', and it is by no means uncommon for another patient to call the chaplain over. While the patient may simply want a chat, *judge* the situation by considering asking her whether she would like a visit from a rabbi or your Jewish colleague if you have one. In asking this question you are respecting the patient's religious identity and what may turn out to be her specific religious and spiritual needs. This is also an example of good teamwork and respecting the work of your colleagues. The fact that the patient is thirsty is a difficult issue, and an *act* may also be refraining from acting. Never give a patient anything to eat or drink without first checking with the nursing staff – the patient may be waiting for an operation or may be 'nil by mouth'. However, if she is not allowed to drink, do at least offer some sympathy, and if you cannot answer any of her questions on this subject, such as how long before she can drink, try and find a member of staff who can.

A visit to A&E can always seem daunting, since you do not know what you will find when you get there. A&E is usually very busy, with staff often rushed off their feet, and at times it is difficult to *see* and grasp the situation. It is also a worrying time and place for patients who may not know what is happening to them and who are surrounded by strangers. It can be very lonely waiting to be seen or waiting for treatment when the outcome is very uncertain. The *act* of spending time with the patient can turn the patient from feeling like a set of symptoms into feeling like a person once again. Moreover, this may be the first time that the patient has faced the difficult questions of illness, disability or dying. In some cases, the chaplain keeps the patient company or deals with practical issues like checking who the patient wants called. On other occasions, the chaplain can be there to help the patient and families when difficult decisions must be made. Sometimes when communication between medical staff and families appears to stumble, particularly over the withdrawal of treatment, the chaplain can clarify the religious position on certain issues or clear up misunderstandings or find another way forward. The answer is to be prepared.

Attending to people who are dying is probably the staple fare of the chaplain. It also asks us to confront our own feelings about dying. *See, judge, act* applies to the chaplain's own personal situation as much as to the situations of other people. We will explore dying, death, grief and bereavement in Chapters 9 and 10. However, when we are faced with worried relatives suffering anticipatory grief, it may be tempting to speak over the person who is actually dying, to talk as if they cannot hear. Certainly, we have to minister to the family. But we also have to remember to *see* the dying person, even if they do not appear to be conscious. Whether or not the person is conscious, their spiritual needs are paramount. The chaplain has a vital role here in affirming not only the dignity of the dying person but also the significance of what is happening to that person as they begin the final part of their journey to God. Family relationships can be quite complex and it is often at the bedside of a dying person that complexities and secrets become clearer or indeed are revealed. In that sacred space at this very sacred time there may be a need for establishing truly healing relationships.

The art of dying well should be the aim of everyone involved in the patient's care. Nursing staff can be particularly sensitive to the needs of their patients, and they are often the first to *see* and *judge* when they recognise symptoms that amount to spiritual distress. Nurses also want to care for their patients professionally and ethically. It may be particularly difficult for a member of staff when decisions are made that conflict with that person's sense of what is right and wrong. Often staff members will turn to the chaplain for moral guidance. We explore end-of-life issues, including the withdrawal of treatment and the withdrawal of food and fluids, in Chapter 9. Chapter 11 deals with issues of conscience.

Nursing staff are no different from any other team, and there may be tensions between people who work closely together. However, the chaplain is not there to take sides. While it is important to *see* the situation for what it is, to listen and to acknowledge people's feelings, it may be more appropriate to suggest a neutral space such as the cafe and to allow a period of time for tempers to cool. Often it is useful to point the staff member in the direction of their own human resources (HR) department. It is important for chaplains to realise that they do not have to deal with absolutely everything themselves.

When there is sudden commotion on the ward, it is not always clear what is going on. In our case study, an elderly and confused man makes a public admission of abuse of minors. From the outset the chaplain should *see* that this is a safeguarding issue and safeguarding is everyone's concern. In particular, NHS staff are trained in safeguarding, and there are certain protocols that must be followed. This is not a question of prejudging a situation before the facts have been established. Nor is it simply good practice. NHS bodies have a statutory duty to ensure they take responsibility and make arrangements to safeguard and promote the welfare of children, young people and vulnerable adults.[1] NHS chaplaincy guidelines remind us that 'where an instance of safeguarding arises during the course of spiritual care the chaplain must alert the patient or member of staff to

---

1   NHS England (2015) *Safeguarding Policy*

the reporting obligations of the chaplain. The policies of the chaplain's organisation must be followed in all circumstances.'[2] We will discuss the boundaries of confidentiality and limits of disclosure in Chapter 4. In our case study, a disclosure has been made in public and before any spiritual care has been offered. The chaplain should be aware of hospital policy on safeguarding, and with the nursing team should follow the procedures laid down. The important thing to remember is that the chaplain is not there to investigate, to discover more, or to be judgemental, and nor can the chaplain make any promises to the person.

Finally, the paperwork: *act*. As a professional responsibility, the chaplain is expected to keep a record of work. The format for this is usually laid out by the chaplain's hospital. Proper record keeping ensures safety, accountability and continuity of care. Chapter 5 deals with questions about data protection and record keeping. By keeping accurate records of referrals and of visits, the chaplaincy team can ensure that patients who have volunteered information about their faith or who have requested support will be seen in a timely fashion. This information also helps with organising shifts and rotas. It also enables the team to reflect on chaplaincy activities. The specifics of actual conversations with patients and other service users remain confidential unless the person asks the chaplain to record particular details. However, it is good practice to record when visits have been made, especially if follow-ups are required.

By the way, did you return to the patient waiting for the test results? Have you organised a visit to anoint the elderly patient?

REFLECTION

Are the basics enough? What would you add? Is it enough just to follow guidelines? How would you prioritise? What does it mean to be professional, even if you are a volunteer or visitor?

---

2   NHS England Chaplaincy Guidelines (2015) *Promoting Excellence in Pastoral, Spiritual & Religious Care*, p.9

A touching question

As one of our five senses, we use touch a lot of the time and sometimes even unconsciously. Touch is also culturally and personally significant – we all know people who love to hug anyone, and people who just about manage to shake another person's hand. However, the use of touch has many meanings. In healthcare, touch is integral to diagnosis, treatment and care where more often than not touch is a matter of procedure. For chaplains, touch is often fundamental to liturgical actions such as anointing or laying on of hands. In everyday life we use touch to attract someone's attention, to affirm them, to reassure them, to show our support, and to show that we care for them and are attentive to their needs. Significantly, touch or the squeeze of a hand can convey far more than words ever could. Touch indeed has a very special place in human interaction. Nevertheless, touch can be misinterpreted or misunderstood. Moreover, touch can also indicate power over another, it can be perceived as a threat or even cause pain. On a practical level a touch can also bring with it germs or infection.[3]

Etiquette, ethics and handwashing?

The prevention of infection is everyone's responsibility, and good hand hygiene has long been recognised as one of the most effective and important measures in prevention. Handwashing then is fundamental to patient care and safety, and so handwashing is also a matter of ethics in the same way as is protecting the rights and dignity of the patient. It may be useful to apply some of the ethical frameworks that were identified in the Introduction to handwashing. Some people wash their hands because the hospital has a rule and insists that protocols around proper hygiene must be followed. Washing hands is seen as an obligation so they wash their hands because they must. Other people look to the

---

3   UK Board of Healthcare Chaplaincy (2010, revised 2014) *Code of Conduct for Healthcare Chaplains*, 4.5

consequences, and if in a particular situation handwashing will result in the most good and least harm, then they will wash their hands. Whether or not they wash their hands depends on the circumstances. Still other people see washing hands as an example of good practice and what the virtuous practitioner would do. They wash their hands, because it is the right thing to do. Other people may decide that washing hands is an example of the caring attitude they should have towards their patients. They wash their hands because they care.

If we apply *see, judge, act* then to *see* means that we have a good grasp of the situation including the circumstances and consequences and can give a description of what needs to be done; to *judge* helps us to reason why, to gather further information and apply hospital procedures and rules; to *act* means that we carry out what needs to be done with the right frame of mind, so that a good action such as washing hands becomes what we always do in this situation.

> REFLECTION
>
> How did you decide? Perhaps you used a combination of these frameworks? Did some of these frameworks have more appeal and others less? Which ones?

Summary

Using the *see, judge, act* approach helps to identify ethical issues, distinguish what is relevant, prioritise where necessary, and seek the appropriate clarifications. For the experienced chaplain, issues such as confidentiality, consent, boundaries and record keeping become second nature. For all chaplains, reflecting on how to apply *POETRY* is a reminder that although the chaplain is a healthcare practitioner, and so shares the ethical concerns of all other healthcare colleagues, the chaplain also represents a faith tradition. The chaplain sees, judges and acts with the eyes of faith.

In accompanying people and responding to their spiritual needs the chaplain is deeply concerned with human beings at often their most vulnerable. We turn next to the patient, their families or carers, and the chaplain's healthcare colleagues as we look at one of the fundamental starting points for healthcare ethics: the dignity of the human person and person-centred care.

Chapter 2

THE DIGNITY OF THE HUMAN PERSON

CASE STUDY

Mrs Elizabeth Smith is 89, and when she had a fall at home her daughter, Jane, called an ambulance. Mrs Smith was taken to A&E where she was assessed. Fortunately Mrs Smith had only fractured her hand, but she was also diagnosed with a urinary tract infection. She was told she would have to stay in hospital for a few days. When the nurse told Jane that 'Betty' did not seem to be very responsive, Jane pointed out that her mother used to be a headmistress in a Church of England school and took a rather formal approach to life. She had never been called Betty, and was also a little hard of hearing so would probably not realise someone was speaking to her.

Jane went home to collect some spare clothes for her mother, and while she was gone, 'dementia' was written in 'Betty's' notes, because she appeared to be confused, unresponsive and disorientated. Jane returned with the clothes, her mother's overnight bag and spare dentures and promised to come back the next day. Mrs Smith was placed in incontinence pads and a hospital gown and transferred to the ward. The following day Mrs Smith tried to go to the toilet, but there was no one available to help her, and the nurse thought it unnecessary since she was wearing pads. Moreover, Mrs Smith could not find her dentures. A porter came to collect Mrs Smith for an x-ray, but since Mrs Smith had not been told where she was going, she became anxious and started to cry. On returning to the ward there was a plate of food waiting for her, but as this had now gone cold and

Mrs Smith was still without her dentures, she declined to eat. When Jane arrived at the hospital, she bumped into the chaplain who said he would come and visit Mrs Smith that afternoon. Jane went to the ward where she found her mother hungry, in tears, in pain from the fractured hand and still in the hospital gown and pads. Mrs Smith had been too scared to ask the nurses for help in case they thought she was being difficult. Then the chaplain appeared at which point Mrs Smith began sobbing inconsolably, asking if she was going to die.

REFLECTION

'Dignity is difficult to define but we know when it is not respected.' Do you think this is accurate? How is dignity related to person-centred care?

Dignity

Healthcare chaplains, like other healthcare professionals, are required to treat those in their care with equal respect and dignity. But what does dignity mean? Some people argue that dignity is now meaningless because it is a vague concept or a concept that can be replaced by more obvious concepts such as autonomy. However, if we look at dignity we shall see that it does have overlapping meanings and that rather than causing confusion, this adds to the richness of the concept as we become more and more skilful in recognising dignity.

In ancient classical times people had dignity if they deserved a particular honour or were held in special esteem, usually because of something the person had done to gain this honour. Today we would call such people dignitaries. Of course, some people had this level of honour purely for who they were – the Emperor, for instance.

Another view is that dignity is intrinsic; that all human beings have dignity not because of what they do or what they deserve but simply because they are human beings. In Christian terms this has been expressed by the understanding that human beings are made in the image of God. This idea of intrinsic dignity can be understood by all whether they are religious or not, and in some philosophies it is explained by saying that we see the other person as another 'I'. In classical notions of dignity, dignity has been bestowed or given to a person and therefore it can be taken away. However, intrinsic dignity can never be lost, and it can never be removed, even if that person is treated in an undignified way. Again, in philosophy, dignity has been expressed by the idea that we are always to treat other people as ends and never merely as means. In recent times, dignity has also been associated with human rights: according to Article 1 of the Universal Declaration of Human Rights 1948 'all human beings are born free and equal in dignity and rights', and there is to be no discrimination between people based on religion, race, gender or creed. Since dignity is associated with the whole person, to respect a person's dignity also includes recognising and preserving the dignity associated with religious and spiritual needs.

We can also speak of other kinds of dignity. There is the dignity of having a particular place in the world and a relationship with others in that time and space in the sense of culture and inheritance. There is embodied dignity, where we affirm our bodily life and existence as a being in the world. There is interpersonal dignity, where we share a common humanity with others. There is a dignity that is expressed in our identity and who we say we are. There is also dignity in the way in which we come to realise that our earthly life is both precious and limited. Dignity, then, can encompass our strengths and weaknesses as human beings.

Although there are many different understandings of dignity, there are two significantly different approaches to dignity. Following the first approach, dignity is empirical, that is to say it has to be actualised or actually found in the person for that person to have dignity. This approach is applied to intrinsic dignity. According to this empirical approach, the human being has intrinsic dignity, because they actually exhibit the characteristics necessary for a human being such as rationality or freedom. This suggests that some human beings do not have dignity because they are not rational or they cannot make choices. Following the second approach, the simple fact that an individual belongs to the human family is enough to ground that individual's dignity. This means that all human beings have human dignity whatever their capacities, abilities or situation.

Dignity is an end in itself and belongs to human beings because they are human beings. Society respects human dignity, and this means that no individual can be sacrificed for the sake of the whole, although there may be exceptional circumstances when a person's interests are infringed for the sake of others – we do, after all, put a person into quarantine to stop the spread of infectious diseases. To acknowledge a person's dignity entails respecting the person's rights, self-esteem, autonomy and privacy, and protecting the person from illegitimate intrusions. Since human beings are both material, bodily beings and spiritual beings, having respect for the dignity of the person also embraces respect for the person's religious and spiritual beliefs and values.

Dignity and person-centred care

It often seems that hospitals by their very nature erode the patient's sense of dignity. Patients are asked to reveal intimate information, including details of their lifestyle. They have to wear institutional gowns and submit to observation and prodding. They follow a routine set by other people's timetables. They are no longer in the privacy of their own homes, and in the ward everyone seems to be able to hear and see what is going on. The chaplain is frequently on the receiving end when the patient's emotions have built up or boiled over. The 'person' of the patient is easily lost in the healthcare system.

By attempting to focus on the patient as a person rather than the service provided, person-centred care developed in part to address the ways in which patients seemed to become objects in the healthcare process. For healthcare professionals to be person-centred they have to be aware of the patient's emotional and spiritual wellbeing, and this is in part why spirituality is the concern of every healthcare professional and not simply that of the chaplain.

The idea of a person-centred approach to healthcare originated from the work of the psychologist Dr Carl Rogers. In the 1950s, Rogers developed a kind of talking therapy in order to increase the self-esteem of his clients. Rogers was convinced that people have within themselves resources to aid their own recovery and he thought that he could achieve better outcomes with his patients if he trusted less in his own expertise and more in patients themselves and their innate tendency to find personal fulfilment. In his person-centred approach to psychotherapy, Rogers identified three core conditions for the therapist: congruence, meaning that the therapist is truly genuine in the relationship; unconditional positive regard, meaning that the attitude of the therapist is one of basic acceptance and support of the patient regardless of what the patient does or says; empathy, meaning that the therapist stands in the shoes of the patient. Rogers argued that these core conditions created a therapeutic climate where people who are accepted and prized develop a more caring attitude to themselves. Instead of focusing on the patient as a patient, person-centred care sees the patient first and foremost as a person who collaborates with professionals in his or her care. Spiritual care is completely person-centred, and it makes no assumptions about the person's own personal convictions or lifestyle.

Although there is now no single definition of person-centred care, this framework of care focuses on treating the person with dignity, compassion and respect with the aim of delivering coordinated, personalised, supportive and enabling care. For care to be properly enabling, healthcare professionals and patients work together, so that what is important to the patient is recognised, so that decisions about care and treatment are made jointly, and so that the patient can identify and achieve their goals. This means that in planning care, healthcare professionals see the patient as an individual with particular needs, desires and values, in their own particular social situation. The patient and the family are seen as partners in planning and decision-making. Person-centred care is about doing things *with people* rather than doing things to them. In general terms, person-centred care has been framed as helping people to have choice and control over their lives and their care; engaging in respectful and listening communication; ensuring good basic care over eating, drinking, pain management and personal hygiene; providing that extra help that gives people independence; respecting people's privacy; making sure they are not isolated.

However, there is a problem if person-centred care is seen as ensuring that everything that is done is based on what is important to that person from their own perspective. What about, say, the person with dementia or with intellectual disabilities or the person who cannot express what is important to them? In the 1970s, Professor Tom Kitwood offered a different perspective on care that came out of his work with people with dementia. Kitwood talks about being person-centred rather than delivering person-centred care. Being person-centred is something we are or feel rather than something we do. Person-centred care is not just individualised good care based on trying to accommodate preferences. In person-centred care we value and respect patients as they are, as unique and individual human beings; we acknowledge their dignity first. Then we attempt to see things from their perspective so that we can offer them genuine support.

Information: person-centred care

Many healthcare institutions have now produced their own healthcare constitutions, standards and guidelines to ensure the delivery of person-centred care, and you can find some of these listed in the Resources section. There have also been patient charters, and in these documents human rights have often been summarised as commitments to fairness, respect, equality, dignity and autonomy. These publications show that there is a growing recognition of the importance of empowering and supporting people to take responsibility for their health. The publications also indicate a commitment not only to patients but also to the public and to healthcare staff.

In terms of care, these publications share some central principles. To begin with, person-centred care is considered to be holistic, and so it includes spiritual, pastoral and religious dimensions. Respect, dignity, compassion and care are seen as key principles, and as the *NHS Constitution for England* explains, these 'should be at the core of how patients and staff are treated not only because it is the right thing to do but because patient safety, experience and outcomes are all improved when staff are valued, empowered and supported'.[1] Valuing the individual person is seen as respect for their aspirations and commitments in life as well as an undertaking to try to understand their priorities, needs, abilities and limits. Some of the guidelines set out lists of legal rights and pledges, such as the right of access to health services, to receive appropriate care that meets needs and reflects preferences, not to be unlawfully discriminated against, to be treated with a professional standard of care, to be cared for in a suitably safe and clean environment, to receive suitable food and hydration. In the commitment to respect the person, certain rights are prominent, notably to be treated with dignity and respect in accordance with human rights; to be protected from abuse, neglect and degrading treatment; to have the right to accept or refuse treatment and if the person does not have the capacity to consent, to be treated according to the principle of best interests; to be given information about tests and treatment options; to have access to their own patient records; to privacy and confidentiality; to be informed about the use of confidential information.

---

1   Department of Health (2015) *The NHS Constitution for England,* p.3

Case study: ethical implications

See: Sometimes a situation appears to require simply practical wisdom, but often ethical attitudes, values and virtues lie behind what is done or left undone. The case study asks you carefully to unravel what has happened and to see what lies behind some of the issues, especially where this is unspoken. Some questions to consider are: do the pressures and constraints of the job justify failures to treat a patient with less than the usual dignity? Is there an issue of ageism here, where certain assumptions are too readily made about a patient's capacities or treatment because of their age? To what extent do we take family concerns seriously?

Judge: When there are many factors to consider, judging helps you to prioritise the events so that you can prioritise your actions. One question to ask is about your own attitudes and conduct.

Act: How do you deal sensitively with colleagues who think that they are doing their best in difficult circumstances? Should someone apologise – if so who?

Some further comments

Healthcare professionals do want to treat their patients with proper consideration and care. However, events often conspire against staff, and patient dignity may be compromised by systemic failures or issues within the organisation. Remember here we are talking about indignities rather than intrinsic dignity. This is more likely to happen where there are problems with staffing levels or bed availability; where elderly patients are placed in acute hospitals which are confusing and do not meet their needs; where care that is task based and therefore in the main responds only to patient requests reduces the patient's sense of independence; and of course time constraints.

Nevertheless, there are some simple things that may appear to be matters of politeness, but are in fact elements that can either shore up or have a negative effect on the patient's sense of self-worth and dignity, and so they also become matters for ethics. Being able to *see* this can make a lot of difference. One obvious thing is to call the patient by their chosen name, and if that means using only their surname then so be it. Consider also what is written up in patient notes. *Judge* carefully. A diagnosis of dementia is not of itself a question of indignity. People live with dementia, they do not necessarily 'suffer' from it and nor are they 'dying from' dementia. Indeed, people can live life to the full with dementia. Moreover, one of the points about intrinsic dignity that can never be lost is that the person always is a person, and is to be treated as a person regardless of condition or situation. Still, the point in the case study is that it is easy to form judgements about people based on things like age or appearance. Good reflective practice challenges us all to think about our preconceptions and question our assumptions.

Anyone going into hospital can feel disoriented and most people have a range of feelings at what is often a vulnerable and disconcerting time. As a healthcare professional, you may wish to consider whether you readily recognise people's emotions, and this includes family members and other members of staff. Once in hospital the patient begins to lose control over what happens: they cannot decide where they are going, when they get up or go to bed, when they eat or what happens next. Patients often feel exposed to the gaze of doctors, nurses and people in the corridor, as they are wheeled past and onto the ward. The traditional hospital gown, open at the back, is perhaps symbolic of this sense of exposure as it is the uniform of the patient waiting for examination. For many people this sense of exposure translates into a sense of lost dignity. Often the *act* of simple good communication can reduce feelings of anxiety, lack of control and disorientation. Good communication helps to build the person up. Ensuring that the person not only is aware of what is happening but also consents to the process is an important affirmation of the person's dignity.

When the chaplain first meets the patient, he may be faced with a range of emotions and feelings before he has had the opportunity to *see* and grasp the situation. It is helpful to be aware that if the patient is not expecting you, your sudden arrival may suggest to the patient that their health is worse than they had expected: the sudden appearance of a priest without warning or explanation may give the patient the impression that the priest has arrived to administer 'last rites' and the patient may mistakenly think that they are dying without being told. Chaplains may be aware of theological thinking on, for instance, the Sacrament of the Sick as a ritual for any serious illness, but as they *judge* the situation they cannot assume that patients are equally aware. A patient whose sense of self-esteem and dignity has been shattered needs to be reassured, they need their self-respect to be restored, they need to be reaffirmed as a person.

The task of restoring balance and dignity is often a delicate one, and an approach that is judgemental of others or that apportions blame is not necessarily helpful. When supporting staff, it is important for the chaplain to recognise what is known as moral distress, where someone knows the right thing to do but the institutional constraints make it difficult or nearly impossible to follow the right course of action. At times, it is also up to the chaplain gently to remind colleagues of the values that underpin their work.

But first consider the times when we have forgotten a person's name, rushed the person through, not listened with care and attention, not thought to explain or communicate, made assumptions about a person's capacities. In short, there have been times when we have not treated a person with respect for their dignity. Undignified care fails to recognise the patient as a person.

Remember perhaps *POETRY*: **p**ray that you always acknowledge a person's dignity; **o**bserve how the person is and be prepared for some remedial work if self-esteem is low; **e**ngage with the person in that sacred space of a person-to-person relationship; give **t**ime so that the person feels affirmed and listened to; **r**emember the person in your prayers and if you meet them again; you also have dignity that cannot be lost even if you fall short of giving dignified care.

As a chaplain, it may be fruitful to think of care not so much as person-centred but as God-centred. After all, if we love God and are centred on him, then we will know how to care for our fellow human beings.

REFLECTION

To what extent, if at all, has your view of human dignity changed? Do you think that dignity is the same as maximising choice?

Ethical communication

Not all effective communication is ethical – I can shout at a person to get that person to do something, but shouting does not usually indicate ethical respect for the dignity of the person. When a chaplain listens and responds to a person who is bereaved, so that a funeral liturgy can be prepared, the communication is effective because the message in the conversation is heard and acted on. However, good communication is more than just an adequate outcome. Ethical communication is honest, open and fosters human worth and dignity. Speaking in clichés, attempting to minimise a person's sense of loss, assuming that you know how a person feels, pressurising a person to talk, can all contribute to a climate of lack of respect. Instead, respect for the person can be demonstrated by open, gentle and sensitive conversation that also includes silence. Three different narrative techniques may be useful here: an external narrative asks the person to tell their story; an internal narrative asks how the person is feeling; a reflexive narrative encourages the person to think about how they are coping and what resources they have.

Ethical communication includes the ability to listen, and good listening involves the ears, eyes and heart. Given that the average person speaks at a rate of about 150 words a minute, and a person can hear at a much greater rate of about 1000 words per minute, we often find ourselves thinking about other things or being distracted while the other person is speaking. This makes for poor listening. There are strategies that you can use to increase your listening skills and to stay focused on what the person is saying – concentrate not only on the words the person uses and on their rate of speech but also on their body language and tone of voice. While the person is speaking to you try not to think about how you are going to respond. Interact with the person with small gestures or affirming words that do not interrupt the flow of the conversation; do not interrupt or finish off another person's sentences.

In order to show interactive listening, paraphrase what the person said to confirm you have not only heard but also understood. Ask for further information where appropriate. Clarify any points that you may not have understood. Remember the important points, so that you can act on them if necessary. Interrupting, jumping to conclusions, making your mind up before you have all the information, talking about your own experiences instead of focusing on the other person, giving advice when it is not asked for, thinking about your response while the other person is speaking are not conducive to building up good listening skills.

Certainly, different situations require different levels of listening. Not listening, pretend listening and partial listening are common everyday ways of listening in human interactions. However, for the most part these three ways of listening are not appropriate in the complex interactions of the ethical healthcare chaplain. Instead, there are further levels of listening that the chaplain may use – in *focused listening*, the chaplain gives his undivided attention; in *interpretive listening*, the chaplain goes beyond simply paying attention to trying to understand what the other person is really communicating; in *interactive listening*, the chaplain shows he is involved by asking for clarification or acknowledging that he understands; in *engaged listening*, the chaplain explores the person's views, values, feelings and interpretations and shares his own. Silence can also be a powerful communication tool, and the chaplain should be aware that silence may convey an unintended or wrong message as well as open up a space for the other person.

REFLECTION

Do you practise listening? Is your listening focused, interactive and engaged?

Summary

We have seen that undignified care depersonalises people. Undignified care disempowers, and it causes the person to become almost invisible. In contrast, dignified care helps the person to maintain a sense of identity even in difficult and confusing circumstances. Dignified care acknowledges the supreme value of the person as a unique individual. Even when undignified care places people in undignified situations, a person can never lose the intrinsic human dignity that belongs to them from the very fact of being a human person.

Person-centred care is frequently related to human rights and often it seems to revolve around the individual's sense of self as a person with needs but also with preferences that should be respected as far as is possible. We turn now to some of the significant though not exclusive supports for human dignity, beginning with autonomy and consent.

Chapter 3

AUTONOMY, CONSENT, REFUSING TREATMENT AND BOUNDARIES

CASE STUDY

Brian has advanced cancer, and his doctors advise him to have surgery and radiotherapy. They say the odds of surviving, albeit with a curtailed active life, are 50:50. Despite pleas from his family, Brian has decided not to go ahead with the surgery or therapy, since he does not want to be dependent or a burden on his family. Belinda, his distraught wife, comes to the chaplain to ask for her assistance in persuading Brian to follow the medical advice. As far as Belinda is concerned, Brian's action is tantamount to suicide.

In the next ward, the chaplain meets Chris who has a degenerative brain condition and is now a wheelchair user. The progress of his illness means that his health will deteriorate, and he will find it more and more difficult to swallow. His mental capacities will remain unimpaired, but he will find it increasingly difficult to communicate. Eventually, Chris may require treatment in the form of artificial hydration and nutrition. Chris is really worried that when he can no longer communicate his wishes the doctors may decide to stop his artificial hydration and nutrition, because they may consider that his life is no longer worth living. Chris asks the healthcare chaplain to help him write up an advance request to demand the treatment that Chris thinks he may need.

REFLECTION

Should autonomy be the ruling principle in healthcare ethics?

Autonomy

In the past, paternalism, often described as 'the doctor knows best', where healthcare professionals take into account their own values in making decisions, was an accepted course of action. This was because it was assumed that everyone shared the same values, patients and professionals alike. However, the situation has drastically changed. Given the great diversity of beliefs and values in today's society, this is often no longer the case and so healthcare professionals must now take the values of patients into account, hence the rise in significance of autonomy of the patient and the importance of informed consent.

There is little doubt that more and more emphasis is now being placed on the importance of the patient's voice and on their rights in healthcare. Healthcare has moved away from the idea that the patient is simply a body to be acted on to the idea that this is the patient's body, and it is for the patient to decide what happens, even if the doctor does know best. However, one of the major questions is whether autonomy should be the sole ethical principle in healthcare. Autonomy may, after all, lead to disastrous results, and a person who decides on a course of action that may cause them serious harm is likely to have their capacity to make such a decision questioned. Moreover, it is important to remember that in a pluralistic culture not everyone sets high store on autonomy – families and heads of households also take part in decision-making. Nevertheless, the value of patient choice is widely recognised, and in the last chapter we saw that person-centred care can be understood in different ways, one of which is to maximise a person's opportunities to follow their preferences. The following of preferences appears to be related to a utilitarian approach to autonomy; that is, an approach which seeks the greatest amount of good over evil where the good is the opportunity for choice. The more choice there is, the better the outcome. Whether choice is right or not is irrelevant.

The word autonomy comes from the Greek *auto* (self) and *nomos* (rule or governance or law). Autonomy has to do with an individual's capacity for self-determination, for making independent decisions and value judgements. Autonomy has different levels: on one level, autonomy means freedom from the interference of others, and in healthcare ethics this usually translates as freedom of the person to make their own decisions free from paternalism or the 'doctor knows best'. On another level, autonomy is to be able to act on the basis of rational principles that the individual has accepted for themselves. On yet another level, autonomy is the ability to reflect on those principles and to transform rules or other principles through public discussion.

However, we may wish to think more deeply about autonomy and preferences. To begin with, consider individual autonomy. Should a decision be made on the basis of the person's immediate desires or choices without further reflection? A patient with a painful arm may ask the doctor to take away the pain by cutting off their arm, but this immediate desire of the patient does not perhaps reflect what the patient really wants. Should we go beyond what the person wants to what they really, really want; that is, the decision reflects the person's overall desires given their own values, even if this is contrary to their immediate desires? But this means we would also have to accept that unreasonable, selfish or self-destructive values may be allowed to play a part in the final decision-making. Perhaps we can think of autonomy as being the author of our own life story? But this is to forget that our story is related to the story of other people; indeed, our stories overlap. One difficulty with a model of individual autonomy is that other people become a threat and in healthcare it seems to lead to a conflict between patient and doctor.

If we do take relationships seriously, then we may wish to consider the autonomy of the doctor. If I can demand treatment that the doctor does not think is in my best interests, does this demand restrict the autonomy of the doctor? If patient autonomy is the leading principle, does this not make the patient into a consumer and the doctor into a service provider? However, consider when the doctor gives information to the patient to inform their choice. The doctor could encouragingly say that an operation has a success rate of 70 per cent, or he could say rather apologetically that the same operation has a failure rate of 30 per cent. The doctor is giving the same information, but arguably he is framing that information and so guiding the patient in their decision-making. On many occasions, instead of making a decision the patient will ask the doctor, or the chaplain, what they would do in the same situation. Can we say that when the patient makes their choice it is truly an exercise of their autonomy?

Finally, we may wish to consider what relationship there is, if any, between autonomy and responsibility. Responsibility involves an awareness of our obligation to make decisions and act appropriately in the light of our commitments to others and to ourselves. The poet John Donne's comment that 'no man is an island' seems relevant here: the notion of autonomy as me being the author of my own life is appealing, but it seems to forget that autonomy is not simply an individual ideal and that autonomy does go hand in hand with responsibility, especially perhaps the responsibility to look after my own health.

Person-centred care is related to enabling choice. Enabling choice and giving consideration to preferences seems to be a way of enshrining autonomy in healthcare. However, when we look at the questions related to treatment, such as consent to treatment, refusal of treatment and whether a patient can demand treatment, it soon becomes clear that autonomy is not an overriding principle.

Autonomy, consent and the healthcare chaplain

Respecting the patient entails respect for their autonomy and this enables the patient to participate genuinely in decision-making. This in turn promotes the patient's value as a person.

To make a decision, the patient requires adequate information. For effective support of the patient the chaplain may also think that he has to be informed about the patient's condition, and we will discuss the issue of information sharing among professionals in Chapter 5.

However, in many situations, especially when there is a crisis, the patient may be overwhelmed and may need time to think about what is happening and what they want. The chaplain has a vital role to play in enabling the patient to move beyond mere choice of one action or another to carefully considered choice; to make not simply a choice but the right choice. The chaplain is well placed and has the necessary professional skills to give time, to engage in attentive listening so that the patient can work out what is possible, what they really, really want, what is important to them, and what they value. The chaplain can also help the patient work through the complexities of the situation, be aware of significant others who will be affected by decisions, and read the new reality of the situation the patient finds themsleves in. Praying with the patient, if the patient wishes, is a vital resource for decision-making.

As with any other patient information, information to do with the patient's religion or spirituality falls under the requirements of consent and confidentiality. We deal with confidentiality in Chapter 5. Patients may give as much or as little information as they choose, and a patient may wish to speak with a chaplain without wanting to disclose anything of their own spirituality, though in this case it would make it difficult for the chaplain to assess the patient's spiritual needs.

Information: consenting to treatment and refusing treatment

When thinking about consent to treatment and refusing treatment, we have to be clear about who is doing the consenting or refusing, because different rules apply to different categories of patients. For instance, there are specific rules when it comes to decision-making with children and young people under 18, and we will discuss these in Chapter 7. The principles surrounding consent and refusal are largely found in common law and in the Mental Capacity Act 2005. Since the Mental Capacity Act has specific application to patients who do not have the capacity to make decisions or patients who are not conscious, but treatment is required in an emergency situation, we will look in detail at some of the provisions of the Act in the next chapter. However, the provisions of the Mental Capacity Act apply to everyone and so we will refer to the Act here as well.

In order to consent to treatment a person must be informed, be free to consent and have capacity to consent. We are talking about patients who are conscious here and so able to respond. For adults over 18, there is no such thing as proxy consent – no one can consent for you, not even a spouse or close family member. Either the patient has capacity for the decision to consent or they lack capacity for the decision. If the patient lacks capacity, then the rules of the Mental Capacity Act come into action and treatment is made not on the basis of consent but on the grounds of the best interests of the patient. The only occasion when another person can consent to treatment on a patient's behalf is if the patient has a valid lasting power of attorney (LPA) under the rules of the Mental Capacity Act and that LPA is put into action because the patient no longer has the capacity to make the decision themselves.

Notice that there is a difference between competence and capacity. Competence is a legal term, and it is generally understood to be the ability to perform actions needed to put decisions into effect. Competence is presumed unless it is determined by a court that the patient is not competent. Capacity is decision-specific. A problem may occur when competence and capacity are confused. We may talk about a person 'lacking capacity', but in fact that person may have the capacity to do all sorts of things, just not the thing we had in mind. When lack of capacity becomes a feature of the person then we forget to look at capacity on a decision-by-decision basis.

In English law, a person who is competent has the right to refuse any treatment, even life-prolonging treatment. Among the very few exceptions to this right are compulsory treatments for very specific communicable diseases such as tuberculosis on the grounds of protecting public health (this does not apply to testing or treatment for human immunodeficiency virus (HIV)) or where a person has been detained under the Mental Health Act 1983 (amended 2007) and the treatment relates to their mental illness. The right to refuse treatment also applies to a woman who is pregnant, even where her decision means that her unborn child will die as well and even where her decision appears to be unwise. The right to refuse treatment is based on common law, which regards treatment without consent as a civil wrong of battery. Although this right might appear to be related to autonomy, it is more about preserving the bodily integrity of the patient – battery damages the body of the patient.

Similarly, the doctor has to seek the patient's consent not so much as an acknowledgment of the patient's autonomy as the doctor's duty to provide the patient with the information they need to make a decision. It is about the professional integrity of the doctor. This is why consent is not merely whether the patient says 'yes' or 'no' and why the doctor has to give sufficient information, so that the patient can weigh the risks and benefits of treatment and any alternatives. In English law there is no right to fully informed consent. Instead, the doctor is not to give too much information such that the patient is confused or unable to decide, nor is the doctor to give too little information so that the patient has no real awareness of what is being proposed. Of course, one problem will always be that of uncertain diagnosis, and a doctor may understandably be wary of telling a patient that they simply do not know since this admission hardly seems to inspire confidence. Perhaps the most satisfactory approach is that the patient is given enough information to ensure that they are not being either deceived or coerced.

While the competent patient has the right to refuse treatment, there is no corresponding right to demand treatment. Notably, in

English law, the provision of artificial food and fluid is considered to be medical treatment (we shall discuss the appropriateness of seeing food and fluid as medical treatment rather than basic care in Chapter 9). The fact that patients cannot demand treatment is usually explained in terms of the injustice that would be caused by diverting resources away from people who need them. However, if we think that doctors should always act in the best interests of their patients, then the doctor would be acting unethically if they gave treatment that they did not think was in the patient's best interests even if the patient demanded it.

In what has been seen by some as an extension of autonomy, the Mental Capacity Act 2005 allows people with capacity to make decisions about treatment they would like to refuse should they lose capacity, and these decisions, if valid and applicable, are legally binding on healthcare professionals if the person does in fact lose capacity. People can also make statements detailing their wishes and feelings about future treatment. Although we will discuss this further in Chapter 4 when we consider ethics and the non-autonomous patient, under the Mental Capacity Act 2005 section 4(6(a)) and section 4(7(a)) the healthcare professional must take account of any statement of wishes and feelings a person may have made.

If treatment is entirely appropriate and in the patient's best interests, then the patient should be able to ask for that treatment, and the healthcare professional should consider that request in the light of the patient's best interests. In deciding best interests, the healthcare professional must take account of the patient's wishes and feelings. If the healthcare professional refuses to give the patient the treatment they request then the patient is entitled to ask for the reason for the decision. There may be good reasons, such as the safety or availability of the treatment. Nevertheless, if the patient remains unsatisfied, they can ask for a second opinion, and even though the patient does not have a legal right to this, most healthcare professionals would rarely refuse. If treatment such as the provision of food and fluids was refused in a deliberate attempt to bring about the patient's death, this would be a serious crime. Healthcare professionals should not deliberately, intentionally and wilfully bring about the death of their patients.

Case study: ethical implications

See: In many situations there are clear ethical issues such as issues of consent and confidentiality. While we often think of consent in terms of the patient and doctor, the chaplain must see that the requirement to obtain consent also applies to her. In addition, these situations may also involve more personal ethical responses that need to be thought through. The chaplain may ask herself what are the real reasons behind the decisions being made? Is either the refusal of treatment or demand for treatment based on an accurate grasp of the situation? How do these decisions relate to cherishing life as a good while recognising that our life on earth is limited?

Judge: While the situations in this case study do have clear legal implications, simply applying legal principles is not an adequate response to the spiritual needs that are evident for Brian, Belinda and Chris. Moreover, the chaplain may like to think how she herself responds to questions of disability, human dignity in apparently undignified situations, conflicts of wishes and resilience in the fact of changing realities. How do you unpick the notion of being a burden? Is refusal of life-prolonging treatment suicide?

Act: Spiritual assessments may help here to clarify what support is needed. However, the chaplain should be aware that not everyone wishes to talk about their spirituality or religious affiliation. Acting ethically and respecting the patient may be a matter of inaction if the patient does not wish to participate in a spiritual assessment. At the same time, the patient may want simply to talk to the chaplain and this is part of good pastoral support.

Some further comments

In the case study, the chaplain seems to be faced with clear-cut situations of one patient failing to cherish his life and the other patient wanting to hold onto life. Both situations concern patients who have firm ideas about what treatment they do not want or do want; both patients are keen to exercise their autonomy. However, if we think of autonomy purely as a matter of personal choice the law appears to favour people who do not opt for life over those who do want life to continue.

In the case of Brian, the chaplain must *see* with a level of caution – after all, the chaplain has been approached by Brian's wife, Belinda, who hopes that the chaplain will persuade her husband to accept the advice of the doctors. As a chaplain you may wonder to whom you are principally ministering; after all, Belinda also has spiritual, emotional and psychological needs. She may be feeling a sense of abandonment or anger or even hurt since Brian seems to refuse to let her care for him. She may also not be ready to lose him so soon. Brian himself does not appear to have asked to see the chaplain and since any inquiry into a person's spiritual needs is stepping into that person's sacred space, the chaplain requires at least consent. Nor can the chaplain assume Belinda's side in persuading Brian. How to provide spiritual care to someone who thinks that the problem lies with someone else requires the chaplain to *judge* boundaries clearly and *act* by looking beyond what one person feels is the problem at hand. To provide effective care for Brian, the chaplain has to *judge* how to gain Brian's consent and then his acceptance and trust; the chaplain has to *act* by first understanding where Brian is coming from and seeing things from his perspective. So prayer is as always first in the order. It may be helpful to avoid rushing in too soon with your solutions and to observe the unspoken when you meet Brian. Feelings of vulnerability often overwhelm patients, and the patient's front of being in control may mask his fear of becoming dependent or worry of being a burden. By sensitive observation the chaplain can reflect on whether the patient's insistent verbal refusal of treatment matches his unspoken body and facial communications. Even the tone of his voice may indicate the sincerity of what he professes.

When you engage with Brian you may wish to consider that there are different approaches to autonomy and choice. For some people, only the patient himself can decide what is good for him. If another person denies the patient his free choice, then this is wrong because it frustrates the good of the patient. The only limit here would be when the free choices of other people are at risk. A different approach may embrace the idea that we are all capable of free choice and of reason and this helps support our intrinsic dignity. But intrinsic dignity is not the same as the actual exercise of free choice. Thinking morally is not simply helping people to choose. Rather, thinking morally is helping people to understand better what is good, so that they can choose the good. Sometimes it is not clear what is the good, though at times this is very clear, and this is one reason why we cannot force the patient to obey the doctor. However, we can help a person identify some basic moral values such as intrinsic dignity that is never lost no matter the person's situation or condition, the option for life as a great gift, and the importance of family and relationships. Taking time helps the person adjust to their new situation. Remember how many people need your help here. Also remember that you may not be the one to 'save' the situation – you may not be God's choice for either Brian or Belinda.

It is not unusual for some people to think that when a person refuses treatment, that refusal amounts to suicide. However, we may first want to ask does the person really will and intend to bring about their death? To think through the idea that all cases of refusing treatment are the same as suicide requires the help of someone who can *see* the situation clearly and *judge* what is being said with compassion. In most cases of refusing treatment, the person decides that the treatment is too burdensome or too difficult, and while they do not aim at an action or inaction that will cause their death, they do accept that death is inevitable. Accepting death, even anticipating that death will come sooner rather than later, is not suicide. (We will consider the ethics at the end of life and what counts as burdensome treatments in Chapter 9.) Although it is right to consider the burdens and benefits of treatments, it is another thing to think that either another person's life or your own life is a burden on others simply because it is a life of dependence. This may require a conversation about our attitudes to disability, our acceptance of the losses that inevitably accompany life, and a recognition of our own vulnerability. As we saw in the last chapter, human dignity does not equal absolute autonomy, and if a person can no longer act as autonomously as they once did, this does not diminish their dignity as a person.

When it comes to the exercise of autonomy, we may wish to think about our duty to care for our health not only for our own sake but also for the sake of others. This means that we should accept some treatments as long as such treatments do not impose heavy burdens on us. Nevertheless, when it comes to treatments that prolong our earthly life, we do not have to accept every treatment at any cost. After all, how we spend our time here on earth is more important than the length of our earthly life.

Unlike Brian, Chris does not think that treatment is burdensome, and he is more concerned that the doctors will stop giving him the treatment he may need, or indeed not even start treatment. Questions that the chaplain may want to explore with Chris may be around the issues of accepting losses, being able to entrust yourself into the care of others and being prepared for death.

Chris wants the chaplain to help him formulate an advanced request for treatment. This request would only come into play once Chris could no longer communicate his wishes, and the doctors would still then make a decision on whether or not the treatment was in Chris's best interests. In practice, a statement of wishes does help to guide those who are making decisions about the care of another person. Under the Mental Capacity Act, to determine best interests the doctors consult family and close friends. This may include the chaplain and so it is wise to make your own written note of Chris's wishes.

Boundaries

Professional boundaries define the identity of the professional, and they enable the person to keep professional and personal identities apart. In situations where there are inequalities of power and vulnerability, such as the situation of chaplain to patient, it is important to maintain boundaries. In the case of chaplaincy, boundaries also involve how much of ourselves we share in our pastoral and spiritual encounters. Meeting and accompanying people rather than taking on a 'fix it' approach, waiting for the other person rather than adopting a parental model to deal with issues, are examples of beneficial boundary setting. Accepting and acknowledging the limits of our competence and making appropriate referrals to other professionals such as psychologists or psychiatrists are also good boundary markers.

Some situations demand very clear and firm boundaries. For example, in cases involving mental health or sexual trauma, establishing boundaries is important for protection and for safeguarding. In other cases there is a skill in getting the balance right. We all unwittingly give signals to others, and there is a skill in maintaining a friendly approach that is also professional. Perhaps a warning sign is when we are tempted to offer a person special treatment. We also should notice when we are going through a difficult time personally, since this may affect the signals we give out. If you are trying to be sensitive to the boundaries of others but are not sure, there is no harm in asking. The safest path to take is to stay within the limits of what you are trained to do and follow guidelines and professional expectations.

> ## REFLECTION
>
> How easy is it to balance autonomy and vulnerability? How difficult is it to discern what I want from what I really want? How do I support patients without imposing my own values, beliefs or practices and how do I respect other people's beliefs, values or spiritual interests?

Summary

Acknowledging the intrinsic dignity of every person, a dignity that can never be lost, is a crucial part of the work of the healthcare chaplain. Respecting the person's own values and beliefs is a part of acknowledging the person's human dignity and their uniqueness as a person. Support for the person's dignity can be found in the way in which healthcare chaplains actively seek out a person's consent to even the most apparently trivial things such as whether the person is happy with a visit. However, consent, the ability to make choices and autonomy are simply aspects of human dignity and being a person. Consent, choice and autonomy do not encompass all there is to dignity. If that were the case, then those patients who were not able to demonstrate their autonomy or choice-making capacities would be devoid of human dignity. The fact that consent, choice and autonomy are not all that is to be said for human dignity is clear in healthcare – autonomy and choice are limited, patients cannot demand any treatment they want, and there are significant protections for people whose autonomy and decision-making capacities are compromised. Given that all human beings, whatever their capacities or situation, have human dignity and the same respect is owed to all, we turn now to ethics and the non-autonomous patient.

Chapter 4

ETHICS AND NON-AUTONOMOUS PATIENTS

CASE STUDY

Mr Jones had a stroke and is now in the rehabilitation unit. He asks the chaplain to come and see him. This is not his first stroke, and he is concerned that another stroke will leave him unable to speak. During the visit Mr Jones confides in the chaplain, and he tells her that he used to have a high-powered job which involved important decision-making. Now he hates being dependent. Moreover, he does not think that his wife would be able to cope if he became more severely disabled. In the event of a cardiac arrest he does not want to be resuscitated, but he does not want his wife to know, in case she thinks that he is giving up.

The chaplain is then called to see if he can help with Cathy, a 25-year-old young lady in distress. Cathy is in hospital for some tests for suspected kidney stones. She has learning difficulties and very little speech, and she was brought into hospital by her mother. Her mother has gone home to collect some clean clothes for Cathy, and now Cathy is upset and wants to leave the hospital. The doctor plans to give Cathy a sedative because of her difficult behaviour.

REFLECTION

How easy is it to identify a person's spiritual needs? How do you identify and address the spiritual needs of a person who you find hard to reach?

Decision-making and non-autonomous patients

In the previous chapter, we explored the importance of autonomy and consent and we noted that in part the move towards respecting autonomy is a move away from paternalism understood as 'the doctor knows best'. We also noted that autonomy is limited. Healthcare professionals, including chaplains, accept that patients can refuse treatment and even make unwise decisions, but patients cannot demand treatment. Moreover, autonomy is not simply about allowing people to make their own decisions. Chaplains have a valuable role in helping people to clarify situations, to see what really matters to them, to address fears that may affect their decision-making, to offer them counsel at difficult times in their lives and help put things into perspective so that they can make the right choice rather than merely any choice.

However, if healthcare professionals were to follow to the line the wishes of a person with serious dementia, or someone who is intoxicated, or in a state of shock and unable to realise what has happened, then the professional may end up doing more harm than good. Does this mean a return to paternalism in the case of a person with diminished capacity?

Part of person-centred care is valuing and respecting people as they are and seeing things from their perspective so that we can offer them genuine support. Person-centred care acknowledges the importance of autonomy and decision-making capacities that people have while nevertheless respecting people whose autonomy is compromised. Authentic care recognises the intrinsic dignity that every human being has regardless of their abilities, capacities or situation. In the encounter with a person whose autonomy is compromised, what should be beyond doubt is that an ethical approach still applies, because ethics is about acknowledging the dignity of the human being.

Information: the Mental Capacity Act 2005

In England, Wales and Northern Ireland everyone over 16 is presumed to have the capacity to make decisions regarding their healthcare and welfare and to be able to consent or withhold consent to proposed treatment. There is no presumption of capacity for people under 16. (In Scotland, the cut-off age is 12.) Unlike people who are over 16, people under 16 have to demonstrate their competence by meeting certain standards that have been set by the courts – in essence, they have to show that they have sufficient intelligence and understanding to grasp fully what is being proposed.

The Mental Capacity Act 2005 came into force in 2007, and it applies to people over 16 years old. The Act has a two-fold purpose: first, it seeks to enable people to make their own decisions as far as possible; second, where this is not possible, it aims to empower others to act in the best interests of the person concerned.

The Act enables a person who has the capacity to make decisions to draw up a legal document called a lasting power of attorney (LPA). This document allows the person to appoint one or more attorneys to make decisions in the person's best interests should the person at some future time become unable to make their own decisions. The Act also enables a person to make an advance decision to refuse treatment, including treatment that sustains life.

In a situation where the patient lacks capacity for a decision, the initial questions to ask are:

- Has the patient got an LPA relating to their personal welfare?

- Has the patient got a valid and applicable advance decision to refuse treatment?

Key principles

There are five key principles which guide how to put the Mental Capacity Act into practice:

1. The Act begins by outlining a presumption of capacity. Under this presumption every adult (over 18) has the right to make their own decisions. The person is presumed to have capacity to make decisions unless it is proved otherwise.

2. Individuals must be supported to make their own decisions. This means that all practicable help should be given to the person, so that they can make their own decisions before anyone treats that person as unable to make decisions.

3. If a person makes what appears to be an unwise decision, this does not mean that the person lacks capacity to make that decision.

4. Any act done or decision made under the Act for a person who lacks capacity must be done in the person's best interests.

5. The least restrictive option of that person's basic rights and freedoms must be chosen.

For those with a mental disorder, the Mental Health Act still applies.

Capacity and advance decisions

The assessment of mental capacity is specific for each individual decision at any particular time. This is to ensure that a person is not treated as lacking in capacity simply because of age or a particular medical condition or disability or diagnosis. The person who assesses capacity is usually the person who requires a decision to be made; for instance, the doctor or nurse.

The test for capacity is in two stages: the first question is does the person have an 'impairment of, or disturbance in the functioning of, mind or brain'?[1] The second question is if the person does have an impairment or disturbance, is that impairment or disturbance sufficient such that the person lacks capacity to make the specific decision? This is a functional test about how a decision is made rather than a question of the outcome of the decision. In applying this functional test, the person assessing capacity considers if the impairment or disturbance means that the person is unable to (i) understand the information relevant to the decision, (ii) retain that information, (iii) use or weigh up that information as part of the decision-making process, or (iv) communicate their decision whether by talking, using sign language or any other means.[2]

'The fact that a person is able to retain the information relevant to a decision for only a short period of time does not prevent the person from being treated as able to make the decision.'[3]

A person with capacity and aged over 18 can:

- appoint an attorney (a named individual, not, for example, a superior of an order) to make decisions in their best interests should they later lose capacity (LPA). An attorney must be a named individual. If the person had previously made an advance directive and then subsequently appoints an attorney, the earlier advance directive becomes no longer valid

- make an advance directive to refuse treatment. If the person wishes to refuse life-sustaining treatment, this needs to be in writing and witnessed

- make other refusals known orally

- make an advance statement or statement of past and present wishes, feelings, beliefs and values that may be relevant when considering best interests.

1   Department of Health (2005) Mental Capacity Act. London: HMSO, section 2(1)
2   Department of Health (2005) Mental Capacity Act. London: HMSO, section 3(1)
3   Department of Health (2005) Mental Capacity Act. London: HMSO, section 3(3)

Advance decisions, statements and any clear oral statements or notes of discussion should be recorded in the patient's file. This is particularly important for the healthcare chaplain, since more often than not a patient will discuss with the chaplain what they do or do not want.

An advance decision, living will or advance refusal should be a clear instruction refusing a medical procedure, intervention or treatment. If this instruction is made voluntarily by an adult who has capacity and is informed, then it has legal force. To be valid it must clearly indicate it is to apply even if life is at risk. However, it must specifically address the situation that has arisen, and it may be invalid if treatment options have materially changed since the patient lost capacity. It also becomes invalid if the person does something inconsistent with the terms of the decision, for instance an advance decision made by a patient who is a Jehovah Witness to refuse blood products may become invalid if the patient changes religious affiliation. It may also be un-enforceable if the refusal puts others at risk of harm. An advance decision cannot override the legal authority to give compulsory treatment under mental health legislation.

A person cannot refuse basic care in an advance directive. This means that treatment for pain relief, hygiene measures and the management of distressing symptoms should be given.

Although legally artificial hydration and nutrition are not part of basic care, basic care seems to include moistening of the mouth and it may include offering food and fluids orally.

If a doctor treats a patient, the doctor is not liable if they have reasonable doubt about the validity or applicability of the advance decision. This might be the case where, for instance, the advance decision was made long before the patient began to suffer from the illness. If the doctor treats the patient where the advance decision is clearly valid and applicable then they are acting illegally even if the treatment would save the life of the patient.

People lacking capacity

If a patient cannot make a decision, and they do not have an LPA or have not made an advance decision, then a doctor or whoever is caring for the patient will make a decision on behalf of the patient. Doctors and carers must take 'reasonable steps' to consult anyone named by the patient about what would be in their best interests, and in general relatives and friends should be consulted. There is a valuable role here for the chaplain, who may be more aware than others of what the patient did and did not want. However, certain medical interventions for a person without capacity are so serious that only a judge sitting in the Court of Protection can make them. Such situations include donation of an organ or bone marrow, and non-therapeutic sterilisation.

An independent mental capacity advocate (IMCA) may be appointed for 'unbefriended people', that is for people who have no relative, friend or unpaid carer to speak for them. An IMCA helps to bring all relevant factors as well as presumed wishes to the attention of the decision-maker, and the IMCA can also challenge the decision-maker where necessary. IMCAs are especially important when serious medical treatments are being proposed or when a significant change to a person's accommodation or stay in hospital has been suggested. IMCAs are also consulted where there are issues of safeguarding and adult protection.

All decisions made for a person lacking capacity must be made in that person's best interests. Under the Act, best interests are not to be determined purely on the basis of age, medical condition or disability but nor is the best interests judgement simply an attempt to determine what the patient would have wanted. The person who determines the best interests judgement should always try and involve the patient as far as possible and should take into account a number of factors, such as, where possible, the patient's own wishes, the views of family members and people close to the patient, the views of appointed attorneys or guardians, and, where there is more than one option, the least restrictive option for the patient. The decision-maker should be clear about their decision and the reasons behind it and in the case of serious decisions the process should be documented.

Of course, there are sometimes difficulties in assessing capacity. It is often assumed that a person lacks capacity even before capacity is assessed, for instance in the case of people with dementia. If someone makes what appears to be an unwise decision or if someone is angry, uncooperative or depressed, it may be assumed that they lack capacity. However, a person may appear to consent to treatment and so have capacity when in fact they do not understand and they are merely complying or seeking approval. As a bridge-builder in communication between people, the chaplain has an important role to play in supporting patients, families and healthcare professionals, in recognising vulnerability and in serving as an advocate where necessary.

DOLS: deprivation of liberty orders

In an emergency, healthcare professionals can deprive an adult who lacks capacity of their liberty in order to give treatment to sustain life or prevent serious deterioration. However, sometimes a patient who does not have capacity for a decision needs to have treatment and the only way in which treatment can be given is to restrict the patient in some way. As a matter of a person's human rights and dignity, no one should be deprived of their liberty, and this includes people who lack capacity, unless there are significant and serious circumstances. Even where such circumstances exist, there must be specific procedures in place so that the person is protected from orders being made without due regard to the circumstances.

In 2014, the Supreme Court considered the issue of deprivation of liberty in the case of *Cheshire West and Cheshire Council v P*. The court ruled that even if a person was well looked after in the best of circumstances and places, that person could still be deprived of their liberty: 'a gilded cage is still a cage.'[4] The court also gave an 'acid test' to aid in the interpretation of deprivation of liberty: (i) Is the person free to leave? This does not mean does the person wants to leave, but would the person be stopped from leaving? (ii) Is the person subject to complete or continuous supervision and control? This test is a matter of simple facts and the whys and wherefores are irrelevant, even if the restrictions are made for positive reasons. If the test is met and the patient does not have capacity to consent, an independent person must review the order and approve it before it can continue. It is important to realise that this does not mean that doctors or nurses are doing anything wrong in restricting a patient. It simply means that an independent person should confirm that the patient's rights are being protected.

Given that DOLs do restrict a patient's rights, they should be avoided wherever possible. They should be authorised only when it is in the patient's best interests and the only way to keep the patient safe. They should be only for a particular treatment plan or course of action. They should be for as short a time as possible.

Life-sustaining treatment decisions

Under the Act, life-sustaining treatment includes the provision of food and fluids (nutrition and hydration). Since decision-makingabout life-sustaining treatment has serious consequences it is important to note that such decisions must not be motivated by a desire to bring about a person's death.[5] On the one hand, some people think that certain categories of patients such as those who are profoundly disabled or those living with severe dementia are 'better off dead'. This means that the removal of treatment, and in particular nutrition and hydration,

---

4   Lady Hale, p.16, para 46, *P v Cheshire West & Chester Council; P & Q v Surrey County Council* (2014) UKSC 19. Available at: www.supremecourt.uk/decided-cases/docs/UKSC_2012_0068_Judgment.pdf

5   Department of Health (2005) Mental Capacity Act. London: HMSO, section 4(5)

is a benefit to them. On the other hand, some people view the withdrawing of nutrition and hydration as unethical. In the Act's Code of Practice 9.61 regarding decisions on life-sustaining treatment it states that the healthcare professional does not have to act against their personal beliefs. But the provision adds that the healthcare professional cannot simply abandon the patient or cause the patient's care to suffer. We will discuss this further in Chapter 9 on the ethical issues surrounding dying and death.

Case study: ethical implications

See: In the complexities of treating patients effectively and lawfully it is easy to lose sight of what lies behind some of the decisions that people make. In order to grasp the situation fully the chaplain must be aware of legislation and of what is and is not possible. The chaplain may wish to consider whether a patient who has capacity does have a clear understanding of the reality of their situation and of other possibilities. In the case of a patient who lacks capacity, the chaplain once again must be aware of legislation. The chaplain should be able to see both the difficulties that her colleagues may be having and also the importance of protecting the rights and dignity of every patient, no matter what that patient's capacity.

Judge: Respect for the dignity of the person is vital, and this includes accepting the person as they are without being judgemental. The ethical concerns of seeking consent and maintaining confidentiality, especially where communication with other people may help to clarify the situation, should be uppermost in the chaplain's mind. Have you thought about what communications skills you can develop to help you be effective in your pastoral ministry?

Act: Often what is required is for the chaplain to be a comforting presence and someone to be relied on. Being with a person rather than doing and fixing is an important ethical action in pastoral care. However, are there also times when you have to stand up for the patient and advocate for them? Can you do this sensitively and without conflict with your colleagues?

Some further comments

It would seem that when a patient confides in the chaplain, then that discussion always remains private and confidential, and we will consider the requirements of confidentiality in the next chapter. However, in the case study Mr Jones tells the chaplain about the treatment he would not want should there come a time when he is unable to express his wishes. With the patient's permission, so that confidentiality is not breached, discussion about what the patient would want must be recorded on file, and this is part of the good practice of *see, judge, act*. The chaplain could also facilitate a conversation between Mr and Mrs Jones about end-of-life care, what they expect and what they hope for, and the reality of care and treatment so that both are reassured that care will be appropriate. One aspect of spiritual care as life is approaching its natural end is *see* – to be realistic about the inevitability of death so that we can *judge, act* and prepare properly. Unless a patient does not want to involve their close family, including family in significant discussions may help to avoid a conflict of views later on and perhaps also avoid the pain caused by thinking that the person could not share their feelings. As a chaplain, you may wish to talk about disability, vulnerability and dependence. For people who are used to being independent, strong and autonomous their pride may be affected by the losses that they now face. Some people do not realise that entrusting themselves to the care of another is one of the greatest gifts they can give to that other person.

Cathy is 25 and so the provisions of the Mental Capacity Act apply to her. The fact that Cathy has learning and speech difficulties does not mean that she does not have capacity to make a decision, and if the doctor thinks that she does have capacity, then the doctor cannot treat her without her consent, nor can the doctor prevent her from leaving the hospital even if the doctor thinks this would be unwise. However, if the doctor is concerned about her capacity and has assessed Cathy to be lacking capacity, then the doctor must make decisions in Cathy's best interests. The presence of a sensitive chaplain may be particularly helpful in this situation. Cathy may be upset because her mother is not with her and she does not understand what is happening. She may simply need a calming presence and time to be reassured until her mother returns. If it is the case that Cathy does have kidney stones, her distress may be caused by pain that has not been addressed. A prayerful moment that takes the form of a calming moment that makes no demands, observation for whatever means she has of communication (and this may mean noticing signs of being in pain), engaging with her on her own terms, giving her as much time as she needs all the while remembering that she may feel alone and abandoned without her mother, may help to reduce Cathy's upset. You may wish to find out more about alternative means of communication for the future and this may be especially useful when it comes to assessing a person's spiritual needs.

Communication

Communication is an ethical issue, because it is not simply about providing information or even seeking consent. Communication helps to establish a relationship with a person, and good communication recognises not only the individuality of the person but also our common humanity. Good communication enables us to treat people fairly, with honesty and with due regard for the situation. Often people with disabilities, people who are elderly or the very young struggle with communication, and it is all too easy for the busy professional to talk down to people, to give them less information, to make decisions without involving them or even to make unwarranted assumptions about them. Indeed, there is a common assumption that some people, for instance those with serious learning disabilities or those with advanced dementia, do not have much of a spiritual life, or at least their spirituality is beyond reach.

Augmentative and alternative communication (AAC) recognises that people use not only speech but other ways of communicating. Sign language is a good example of ACC; however, ACC need not be so specialised. In fact, we use AAC when, for instance, we use a gesture or point to something, make a facial expression, use symbols or pictures or write. Some people are adept at eye pointing – the person will look intently at something and hope that you have noticed that this is something they want. Some people use particular aids to communicate, such as laptops, apps on their mobile devices, or symbol and picture boards. A person with learning difficulties may not realise that you do not know they do use such devices so it may be up to you to find out from family or carers or from your own observations.

In general, conversations are better held in a quiet place where both you and the person can concentrate. Ask if there is anything specific that may help you both and as long as the person feels comfortable, make eye contact with them. This will also help you to notice their body language or gestures. Be prepared to have patience, to keep it slow and to wait for a reply, but start perhaps with the current situation and how the person is feeling: simple emojis or smiling or unhappy faces might be enough to make that initial connection.

> **REFLECTION**
> Has your view of dignity changed (again)?

Summary

Human dignity underpins the idea that autonomy, and decision-making is an important aspect of being human. However, the lack of capacity to make decisions does not undermine or diminish human dignity. We are all fragile human beings in different ways and just as independence is an aspect of human nature, so too is dependence.

We now turn to some significant supports for human dignity that apply to all in a healthcare setting: confidentiality, privacy, data protection, truth telling and trust.

Chapter 5

CONFIDENTIALITY, PRIVACY, DATA PROTECTION, TRUTH TELLING AND TRUST

CASE STUDY

In the lift the chaplain finds herself chatting to Eva, a doctor she knows well. Eva is especially concerned about her elderly patient, Mrs Dawson, whose recent scan results show signs of advanced cancer. Eva is planning to break the news to Mrs Dawson later that afternoon, and she suggests that Mrs Dawson would appreciate a visit from the chaplain, since the chaplain has already been involved in her care. Indeed, the chaplain has also met Mrs Dawson's family. To ensure she is up to speed on the case, the chaplain checks for further information about Mrs Dawson on her hospital electronic record. Then in the corridor, the chaplain meets Mrs Dawson's two sons, Fred and Greg, who are on their way to visit their mother. The chaplain offers her sympathy on the diagnosis. Fred and Greg are dismayed at this news and they discuss whether or not it would be wise to tell Mrs Dawson the results of the scan. Fred and Greg are worried that their mother may give up hope, so they ask the chaplain to promise that she will not tell their mother what she knows and instead say that everything is alright. At Mrs Dawson's bedside the chaplain is careful to maintain patient privacy by carefully drawing the curtains. Later that day, as she is writing up her visiting record, the chaplain reflects that Mrs Dawson's case would be a useful example for a presentation she is giving to the parish community on hospital chaplaincy. That evening over dinner she discusses this idea with her husband, Harry.

REFLECTION

Is it easy to keep confidentiality?

Privacy

We have already seen the importance of personal dignity and person-centred care. Preserving a patient's sense of privacy is a part of respecting that person's dignity. In practical terms when meeting a patient this includes ensuring that the person is comfortable, that doors or curtains are partially closed (it is advisable to leave a gap in curtains and doors ajar for staff access) and that a sense of private space is maintained. Privacy involves anything about a person that could become public. Confidentiality is more to do with relationships, communication and information. When a person discloses personal information, they have already given up a little of their privacy, and generally this is done on the understanding that this private information will be kept confidential.

Confidentiality

When a person discusses their health with a healthcare professional, including a chaplain, it is reasonable for them to assume that anything they say will be held in confidence. At first sight this may seem to be simply a private matter of trust between the patient and the professional. However, confidentiality is also a public matter of trust. After all, it is in the public interest that people have the confidence to seek appropriate treatment and share relevant information. Healthcare professionals have a duty to preserve confidentiality. Information that is given in confidence should be kept confidential, unless there is a compelling reason why it should not be or unless the individual has consented to personal information being disclosed.

The kind of information that should be kept confidential includes anything that might identify the patient, whether written down or not; any pictures, photographs, other images or audio recordings of the patient; any clinical information about the person's diagnosis or treatment; information about who is the person's doctor or which clinics the person attends; anything that either directly or indirectly could lead to the person being identified if that information is used alongside other information such as a date of birth or postcode. When information applies only to a very small population, for instance, a rare disease, additional care must be taken to ensure that individuals cannot be identified.

However, confidentiality is not an absolute principle and it does have limits. In some situations, healthcare professionals have a legal duty to disclose information given to them in confidence. The professional must not disclose more information than is necessary and disclosure must be made to an appropriate person. Where there is such a legal requirement the individual concerned does not have to consent, but they should be made aware of the disclosure and be assured that the information will be kept secure.

A chaplain should not disclose confidential information unless the disclosure is in the patient's best interests and the chaplain has explained the need to share the information and the patient has agreed. If all of these conditions are satisfied, then the chaplain can disclose the information but must do so in a secure way and to the appropriate person. Leaving text messages, voicemails or messages on an answering machine are not considered to be secure methods of passing on information.

An exception to keeping information confidential is where there is a serious risk of self-harm or harm to another person or the suggestion of a crime (for instance, child abuse). If you are made aware of any of these kinds of information, then you should advise the person that you have a duty of care to ensure that the information is shared with the appropriate person (this may be the ward sister, the patient's doctor or the lead chaplain). Wherever possible, try to encourage the person to disclose the information themselves.

We may want to ask whether chaplains should adhere to a stricter standard of confidentiality than other healthcare professionals. After all, the secrecy of the confessional is often associated with clergy, and patients may simply not expect chaplains to divulge conversations about spirituality or emotions or matters that make patients particularly vulnerable. Certainly, confessional information is privileged. Non-confessional information may be shared because, as with the sharing of any patient information, it still remains subject to the professional standards of confidentiality and data protection. However, chaplains do need to exercise prudential wisdom and be attentive to the patients' best interests as patients themselves understand them, including their privacy over sensitive matters. The space between chaplain and person is indeed sacred, and the conversation in that space should be handled with care. Sometimes a verbal conversation over a sensitive issue is preferable to documentation: remember that patients can now have access to their own notes and they may not wish to read over times of their own vulnerability.

Data security

The question about whether a hospital chaplain should have access to patient records is an interesting one. If chaplains are not regarded as full healthcare professionals or members of the healthcare team, then it would seem that chaplains should not have access to patient records. If chaplains are seen only as religious ministers, then patients may not expect chaplains either to read their records or to have conversations with medical practitioners. However, the healthcare profession increasingly sees patient care as multidimensional and it recognises that chaplains are often uniquely placed to glean information, whether it be psychological, social or spiritual, that can help in patient care. Moreover, the fact that chaplains do provide data and documentation about their activities, and in particular carry out spiritual assessments, shows that they participate fully in the healthcare profession.

Having patient information accessible is important for effective care. Yet it is equally important that patient information is kept confidential, and this means that it is safe from access by those without authority to see, hear or read it. Patient information should be secure against loss or breaches of confidentiality, and it should retain its integrity. This means that it is protected from unauthorised alteration or damage. There should be no conflict between protecting and sharing information. Sometimes there are difficulties in keeping data secure, especially when chaplains do not have their own office or computer or access to a data security system. Nevertheless, data security is a concern for everyone working in healthcare.

Keeping data

Keeping data is becoming an ever more important part of working practice. Data keeping forms a part of a monitoring process that ensures quality practice. Data can show that chaplains are adhering to appropriate legal requirements and it illustrates examples of good practice that can be shared with others. Data analysis helps to formulate, establish and maintain good standards of care.

Keeping data also generates research, and being aware of current research is a significant part of good reflective practice. Sharing evidence-based practice helps chaplains to identify good and less good ways of working, and it helps them to develop more a more effective ministry. Some of this evidence comes in the form of models of service, guidelines and standards of practice for chaplains. Chaplains are also encouraged to collect and record their own data on their activity. Certainly, the nature of chaplaincy means that sometimes this is difficult to do – often the chaplain is involved in chance encounters, and spiritual care is frequently given in informal settings and circumstances. However, there are specific occasions when it is relatively simple to note what you have done, and this information can be used to help you plan your time, to demonstrate where the needs for chaplaincy are, and to show to your employers that your work is of value. You can collect this information in the format of a diary entry made during each working day and collated into a weekly summary, so that you have your own minimum data set. The kinds of occasions to note down include:

- all call-outs you have when you are on call

- all call-outs you have on your normal visiting schedule

- all visits that you make after a referral from people outside your department, such as those from patients, relatives, staff and religious colleagues

- all occasions when you have provided religious rites or given the sacraments

- all visits involving prayer

- all the times when the client cries or shares spiritual pain or concerns about life, or the search for meaning, or even thanks you for a visit

- all visits where further action is needed, for instance by another team member

- all visits to internal staff or outside people or agencies

- occasions where you act in the capacity of an advocate

- occasions where you are asked for specialist knowledge.

Keeping your own diary of your chaplaincy activity is also a useful personal resource. Keeping your own notes can contribute to good patient care because notes will act as a helpful way of seeing at a glance who needs a visit, and your notes will ensure that people do not get lost in a busy the week. Your diary will also let other people know the extent of your work. This will help in any appraisal of your work and in being accountable to others, whether patients and relatives or colleagues.

Truth telling

Being honest, trustworthy and acting with integrity are part and parcel of being a healthcare chaplain. Some 50 years ago it was common for doctors to keep the truth from their patients with the best of intentions. Doctors thought that they were sparing patients from distress – at one time many patients understood that a diagnosis of, for instance, cancer implied a painful death sentence. Of course, there are some people who do not want to know the truth of their condition and that is to be respected. However, there is a difference between concealing or distorting the truth and using careful language that does not frighten the patient but does convey meaning. For many people, health may be important but it is not the only or even the greatest value. People do value relationships, getting their affairs in order, dealing with unfinished business, deepening their spirituality and relationship with God. If there is no truthfulness, there is no real relationship between the patient and the chaplain. Moreover, deceiving someone may be failing to treat that person with the respect owed to human beings. The chaplain has a particular role to play in helping people come to terms with what is happening to them, to clarify what is important to them, to address their spiritual needs, and for these reasons prudential truth telling becomes crucial.

Healthcare professionals also make mistakes, and truth telling in these circumstances is important, so that if possible, things can be put right or at least assurances made that the cause of the mistake will be investigated thoroughly and properly, with no cover-up.

Of course, doctors know only too well that we live with uncertainty. Some things can be clearly identified such as cancer or kidney stones. But the medical profession also recognises that there is an element of the unknown, especially when it comes to prognosis. Prognosis is a matter of statistics, and the range may be wide. The chaplain is well placed to allow patients to ask the questions that they want to ask, to explore options, to question what they really, really want. The chaplain can also offer hope and not only the realistic hope of palliation. Sensitive and clear communication can help patients and their families understand how illness is affecting them, how they can have some control over the choices open to them and how to make plans. This communication can lead to a real accompanying of the person because our ending is a very important part of our spiritual wholeness.

Information: handling patient information

Handling patient information and keeping data secure is becoming more and more complex, especially with the advent of electronic records and data-sharing programmes. Healthcare chaplains should be familiar with the principles found in two important documents regarding the handling of patient information: the Caldicott Report of 1997 and the Data Protection Act 1998.

Caldicott Report

In 1997, Dame Fiona Caldicott chaired a review of how patient information was handled across the NHS. The review formulated what became known as the Caldicott Principles. These six principles, with a seventh principle added in 2013, ensure that information is protected and used only when appropriate.

- *Principle 1:* Every proposed use or transfer of personal confidential data must be justified, clearly defined and documented, and if it is continuously used, it must be regularly reviewed by an appropriate person.

- *Principle 2:* Any personal data that is included must be essential for specified purposes, and personal data cannot be used unless it is there. The need to identify patients should also be considered at each stage of considering the specific purpose.

- *Principle 3:* Only the minimum amount of personal data necessary should be included.

- *Principle 4:* Access to personal confidential data should be on a strict need-to-know basis.

- *Principle 5:* All those who handle personal confidential data should be aware of their responsibilities and obligations regarding patient confidentiality.

- *Principle 6:* Every use of personal confidential data must be lawful, and there should be someone responsible for ensuring that the organisation complies with legal requirements.

- *Principle 7:* Sharing information in the best interests of patients should take place within the framework of these principles, since the duty to share information can be as important as the duty to protect patient confidentiality.

Large health organisations are encouraged to appoint a 'Calidcott Guardian' to act as the 'conscience' of the organisation and to enable ethical and legal sharing of information according to the Caldicott Principles.

The Data Protection Act 1998

The Data Protection Act 1998 sets out the responsibility of healthcare professionals to keep data secure and private, and to ensure that data is only used in order to provide good healthcare. The Data Protection Act also gives people the right to view information an organisation holds about them.

The Data Protection Act outlines eight important principles regarding personal data:

- *Principle 1:* Personal data must be processed fairly and lawfully.

- *Principle 2:* Personal data shall be obtained only for one or more specified purposes.

- *Principle 3:* Personal data must be adequate, relevant and not excessive in view of the specified purposes for which they are processed.

- *Principle 4:* Personal data must be accurate and, where necessary, kept up to date.

- *Principle 5:* Personal data must not be kept longer than is necessary for the specified purposes.

- *Principle 6:* Personal data must be processed in accordance with the rights of data subjects under the Act.

- *Principle 7:* Personal data must be kept secure, and appropriate measures will be taken against unauthorised or unlawful processing of personal data and against accidental loss or damage to personal data.

- *Principle 8:* Personal data must not be transferred to countries outside the European Economic Area, unless there are adequate levels of protection, and security can be ensured.

Case study: ethical implications

See: Having a good grasp of the situation involves knowing the parameters of good practice. Knowing about data protection, consent and confidentiality will ensure that the chaplain stays within those parameters. However, ethics goes beyond simply applying protocols. The chaplain may wish to consider what lies behind a request not to tell the truth to a patient. Where the chaplain is giving pastoral support to several people in the same family or on the same case, is it easy to see how to unpick the different and sometimes competing needs and requests?

Judge: We all need to talk. Do you know who you can talk to and about what? How significant is truth telling? We may be aware of issues of privacy such as closing curtains, but have we got our priorities right if we fail to respect confidentiality?

Act: In order to act ethically, competently and professionally, a chaplain should be clear on the specific requirements of consent, confidentiality, privacy, data protection and truth telling. Are you?

Some further comments

Anyone can make a referral to the chaplaincy team, and it is good practice for the chaplain always to check that patients are happy to receive a visit. It would seem that Eva acted appropriately in suggesting that the chaplain visit Mrs Dawson. However, there is a question over maintaining patient confidentiality and privacy. The chaplain may wish to *judge* whether these may have been compromised by the extent to which Eva discussed Mrs Dawson's case and the details she offered to the chaplain even though the chaplain was already involved in Mrs Dawson's care. One useful test to *see* when health professionals share information is the 'no surprise test' – information should not be shared in ways that the patient would be surprised to learn about. Perhaps more significantly, people often inadvertently treat public spaces as private and any disclosure of confidential information during informal conversations in public spaces such as lifts or corridors does not seem to conform to privacy requirements.

Any information given in the course of a pastoral conversation is confidential. The chaplain can only use the information for the purpose for which it was given, and in the case study this appears to be only a referral for a visit. Moreover, the chaplain should not seek to obtain any other information about a patient from any other source, unless the patient has requested that the chaplain does so *and* it is in the patient's best interests. Information about a patient, whether it is about admission, diagnosis, treatment or even which ward the patient is on, should not be given to a third person, and that includes family members, unless the patient has asked you to give that person the information. Having shared the diagnosis information with Mrs Dawson's sons without her knowledge, and so therefore without permission, the chaplain is now in a difficult situation and this difficulty may also extend to Eva, whose job it was to give the diagnosis to her patient in the first place. The chaplain has to support Fred and Greg at this difficult time and take account of their concerns for their mother. However, it is not helpful to be in a situation where a person demands promises that the chaplain cannot or even should not keep. The chaplain would be wise to make this clear to Fred and Greg and explain that she is also there to support Mrs Dawson. Gently explaining the importance of truth telling, especially when it comes to making practical and spiritual preparations at the end of life may be a way forward. Their mother may be more resilient than Fred and Greg give her credit for. An essential part of good support is making an assessment of spiritual needs, and this requires the patient, their family and the chaplain to *see* the situation clearly by grasping what is happening and knowing the truth of the situation, to *judge* priorities and what must be done, and to *act* appropriately.

Being able to link theory with actual situations is part of research, reflective practice and the dissemination of good ways of working. However, as the expression goes 'it is a small world', and the world of the faith community may be even smaller. Anything that identifies a patient or hospital would be a breach of patient privacy. However, stories composed of several cases may equally illustrate the intended point without privacy being compromised.

At the end of the day most people like to unwind, and it is not unreasonable for people to want to talk about challenging moments in their day. Everyone needs someone to confide in. Once again, the chaplain must exercise prudential wisdom in the extent to which she discusses her work with those outside the hospital, even her own family. The advantage of the chaplaincy team is of course that a chaplain has an appropriate person to confide in. After all, the chaplain also needs a chaplain!

Perhaps the chaplain could apply *POETRY* to her own situation. **P**ray as always. **O**bserve the requirements of privacy, confidentiality, data protection and truth telling conscientiously. **E**ngage with the relevant policies and procedures, including the core competencies of healthcare chaplaincy. **T**aking proper **t**ime over matters will ensure there are no rushes that may lead to risking these requirements. **R**emember you are a professional and have professional standards. **Y**ou do matter and so does your own integrity.

Privacy, confidentiality and the person who lacks capacity

We have seen that any disclosure of information to relatives or to third parties requires the consent of the patient. But what if the patient lacks capacity to consent? Does this mean that ethical considerations no longer apply? If a patient is judged to lack capacity, then any decision is to be made in the best interests of the patient. However, health professionals may need to share information with relatives and people close to that person. This is because under the Mental Capacity Act in assessing best interests, the decision-maker is to take account of the views of relatives, carers, friends, advocates and people involved in the patient's care. Health professionals need not attempt to seek explicit consent from the patient, and often this may be impossible. However, this does not mean that the healthcare professional can simply and routinely share information. The professional should exercise sensitivity and prudential wisdom in making a decision about how much and what information the patient would like to be shared and with whom. If there is evidence that the patient did not want information to be shared then this should be respected.

REFLECTION

How can some disclosures be healing and how can the chaplain facilitate this (without compromising confidentiality)? Do you think that confidentiality, privacy, data protection and truth telling are matters of justice? Why?

Summary

Issues of privacy, confidentiality, data protection and truth telling are not simply private matters concerning the personal integrity of the chaplain and the personal life of the patient. These are matters of public trust and they reflect the ethical standards of the healthcare profession. For chaplains, as for all healthcare professionals, respecting privacy and keeping confidentiality, while also recognising the limits of confidentiality, are clear indicators of upholding the dignity of the patient as a person.

We have talked so far of the patient as an adult and the dignity of the patient as a person. What about children and babies? They have the intrinsic dignity that belongs to every human being just by being human. However, that leads into another question for ethics: when does the human being begin?

Chapter 6

ETHICAL ISSUES AT THE BEGINNING OF LIFE

CASE STUDY

Alison is devastated. She is expecting her first baby, and following the initial scan the doctors are concerned that there may be something wrong with the baby, so they want her to go for more tests. Alison's parents think that she should decide whether she wants to have a termination and the sooner the better. After all, she is young and can always have another baby. Moreover, they say that Alison would be wrong to bring a disabled baby into the world, because it is bound to suffer, and it will make family life so much harder. Alison goes to the chaplain for advice.

Meanwhile, the chaplain has been called to see Bill and Caroline whose unborn baby is at 27 weeks' gestation. The baby has been diagnosed with a condition that the doctors say is incompatible with life, and they have recommended a termination. Bill says that he has been made to feel that a decisive action to terminate the pregnancy will end their nightmare but a decision to continue the pregnancy is 'copping out' and a bit like a decision to do nothing.

> ### REFLECTION
> What does your faith tradition have to say about the beginning of life?
>
>   'You can always have another': Are babies replaceable? Should society protect a human being from the beginning or at some other stage in their life? Why?

When did I begin?

When we think of ethical issues at the beginning of life, decisions concerning newborn babies may first spring to mind, and this will form part of the subject of our next chapter. However, science tells us that the beginning of life happens some nine months before birth. Moreover, the media frequently reports on a huge number of issues surrounding reproductive ethics such as IVF, surrogacy, donation of sperm and eggs, cloning, stem cell research, 'designer babies', pre-implantation diagnosis, to name but a few. In addition, there are the controversial questions of embryonic stem cell research, pregnancy testing and screening for disability, and abortion (termination of pregnancy). Chaplains may find themselves involved in any one of these. These controversial questions do invite reflection on when life begins. While some people may think that life begins at birth, we know from technology that the foetus is 'alive and kicking' long before that.

    Since we cannot deal with all these questions, we will look at the ethics surrounding two issues that the healthcare chaplain is likely to encounter: pregnancy testing and abortion or termination of pregnancy. Abortion is a particularly contentious question, and in situations where healthcare chaplains are acting as representatives of their faith tradition, it is important that they know where their faith tradition stands on this issue. Many religions take a strong position on abortion, simply because abortion involves the killing of a human being. However, many religious traditions also recognise that abortion concerns not just the new human being and their family but also our relationship with God as Creator of life. This makes it more difficult and ultimately inadequate to think about abortion and the embryo in purely intellectual terms. Moreover, chaplains rarely deal with people who see the issue simply as an intellectual conundrum. Good people struggle with the tragedy of abortion. Not only do different faith traditions have different views on abortion and the embryo, there are different positions within some faith traditions, even if a broad generalisation can be given. To take but a few, the Church of England is strongly opposed to abortion, yet it recognises that there are conditions, albeit strictly limited, where abortion is preferable. The Roman Catholic Church holds that the deliberate, direct and intentional killing of an embryo at any stage from conception is a grave wrong. In Islam, abortion is rarely permitted after 120 days or after ensoulment, unless the mother's life is seriously in danger, though some Muslims permit abortion on the grounds of disability of the foetus. In Judaism, abortion may be permitted for serious reasons, for instance to save the life of the mother. However, to begin with it may be useful to reflect on one thing: the human embryo.

When we are thinking about the human embryo, it may be helpful to consider what it is before thinking about how it is to be treated. We may start by asking: is it human life? When an egg cell and a sperm cell fuse at fertilisation, a one-cell zygote is produced, and this life is not that of just its father or its mother. This single cell brings about its own developmental changes by dividing many times, forming many cells that gradually become different from each other, forming for instance the nervous system, the circulatory system, heart and other organs, and the brain. Growing, developing, changing, while remaining the same, the zygote is called an embryo, and then at about week six of gestation, it is called a foetus. The six-week foetus already has its own blood system and might even be a different blood group to its mother. Since fertilisation usually occurs in the secret space of the mother, the exact date of fertilisation is not known, and so in the UK pregnancy is calculated from the first day of the woman's last period, and the average pregnancy lasts about 280 days.

Some people argue that although the embryo is human life, it is not *a* human life, meaning it is not an individual human being. This argument is carried on three particular grounds: first that it does not look like a human being; second, some of the cells in the embryo develop into the placenta or umbilical cord; third, in a small number of cases and in the first 14 days or so after fertilization, the embryo may divide resulting in two or three or more individuals. Certainly, it is true that the early embryo does not look like a fully grown human being, and it does not even look like a baby, since it does not have distinct features or limbs. However, it has to be said that it does look like a human being who is of one-day or one-week gestation – this is what I looked like at this stage of my development, and I am a human being. The argument that the embryo is not just an individual, because it also contains cells that become the placenta is also true. However, this argument seems to forget that the embryo and placenta develop jointly as a functional unity. The argument that the embryo is not an individual because it may be two or three individuals in the future is interesting. We may wish to ask, if we cannot establish how many individuals there are, does this entitle us to conclude there are no individuals? Moreover, if there is the possibility of more than one individual, does this not make the early embryo even more precious?

A further argument points to the fact that many embryos perish naturally during the developmental process and often the woman concerned is not even aware of this loss. The argument continues by asking if nature is not concerned then why should we be? Of course, the counter argument is that we are naturally concerned and that is why we acknowledge the tragedy of miscarriage or babies that do not make it to birth. Other people argue that even if the embryo is a human life, the individual that is me, 'I', begins later on in the process, for instance when I have a soul or when I become a person or have self-consciousness. These of course are difficult theological and philosophical questions, but we can see that moral or ethical considerations, the moral status of the embryo or how to treat the embryo, depend very much on what we think the embryo is. And science appears to tell us that from conception human development is a continuous process.

Current technology and in particular the development of non-invasive prenatal testing (NIPT) raises some significant ethical questions. On the one hand, society values the importance of access to good information and choice for pregnant women and couples. On the other hand, all human beings whatever their condition, situation, or ability are equal in dignity. Society is recognising more and more that people with disabilities can live life to the full. One major question we have to consider is the extent to which NIPT changes how we see pregnancy and its apparent medicalisation, and how we view disability and difference. With advances in technology, tests in the future may be able to pick up conditions that have their onset in adult life. In NIPT, disability is screened out by the termination of a foetus that is diagnosed as having a particular disabling or undesirable condition. As some people who speak on behalf of people with disabilities point out, there is less incentive to work on finding cures for disability or finding ways to support people who are disabled, and there is more risk of discrimination if the solution to disability is to eradicate the disabled foetus.

Information: testing and screening in pregnancy

Non-invasive prenatal testing is an accurate method of testing for different genetic conditions and features, though there remains the risk of some false positive results. NIPT, such as ultrasound scans and blood tests, is routinely offered to pregnant women and different tests are offered at different stages of the pregnancy. Research suggests that women accept screening because they perceive it to be a routine part of antenatal care rather than women making an active choice for screening. Scans are completely painless, they have no known side effects and they do not harm either the mother or the foetus. The first scan is usually offered at between eight and twelve weeks. Based on the baby's measurements, the sonographer (a specially trained professional) can estimate when the baby is due and check the positioning of the baby. This scan also will show if there is one or two or even more babies. Most expectant parents are excited at the prospect of having a glimpse of their unborn baby, albeit as a grainy black and white image. However, parents should be aware that scans may also detect abnormalities or problems. The first scan is often combined with a blood test and this combined test assesses the chance of the woman having a baby with Down syndrome. The first scan can also assess for the risk of Edwards syndrome or Patau syndrome. The scans themselves cannot tell for certain if the baby has any of these syndromes, nor can scans pick up every problem. If the scan suggests that there may be a possible problem, further diagnostic tests may be offered. These diagnostic tests are more invasive and carry the risk of miscarriage. The second scan that is offered between 18 and 21 weeks pregnancy checks the baby's size and whether it is growing properly. It also checks for abnormalities (anomalies) in the baby that only show at this stage.

Routine scans and further tests can be useful, so that if necessary a multidisciplinary plan for management of the pregnancy and birth can be put into action. More invasive tests, particularly those with a risk of miscarriage, need to be carefully considered. Sometimes women feel pressurised into making quick decisions. They forget that they can talk to professionals and ask additional questions, although it is also important to realise that further tests are optional. Moreover, the actual situation may not be clear early on and indeed may remain uncertain until the baby is born; some conditions are fatal, some serious, and some may require surgery or other treatment. In other cases, for instance a diagnosis of Down syndrome, there is no way of knowing how the baby will be affected. However, knowing about the risk of a disability can help pregnant women, couples and extended family to prepare for the future. Prenatal screening may give extra information and so help with decision-making, but we should all also get to know about the rich and varied lives that people with disabilities lead. There is a serious ethical question about the prevalence of common negative attitudes to disability and sometimes it is worth pointing out that having a child with disabilities can enhance family life in the same way as having any child would.

Termination of pregnancy

In the UK, under the Offences Against the Person Act 1861 sections 58–59, it is a criminal offence for a woman to attempt her own abortion or for another to assist in attempting an unlawful abortion by any means whatsoever, even if the woman is not pregnant. Following the Infant Life (Preservation) Act 1929, if a pregnancy has lasted for 28 weeks, the foetus is presumed to be 'capable of being born alive', so termination would be child destruction. The provisions of the Offences Against the Person Act mean that abortion is a criminal offence. However, the Abortion Act 1967 sets out certain conditions that provide extensive defences to any criminal charge. This also means that there is no right to abortion, nor, strictly speaking, does a woman have a right to choose to have a termination.

All those who are involved in providing and commissioning treatment for termination of pregnancy need to comply fully with the requirements of the Abortion Act 1967. There are four requirements:

1. The termination must be carried out under the authority of a registered medical practitioner. Once a doctor has decided that there are grounds for termination, other professionals can carry it out.

2. A termination can only be carried out in an NHS hospital or another approved place.

3. Two medical practitioners must agree that one of the statutory grounds permitting abortion may be applied.

4. All abortions must be notified to the relevant authorities.

Unless an emergency abortion is required under section 1(4) of the Act, a pregnancy may only be terminated if two registered medical practitioners certify that in their opinion and based on their good faith, at least one of the grounds for abortion from section 1 of the Act exists. The practitioners must agree on the grounds. Under the Abortion Act section 1, amended by the Human Fertilisation and Embryology Act 1990, the grounds for abortion are:

- 'that the pregnancy has not exceeded its twenty-fourth week and that the continuance of the pregnancy would involve risk, greater than if the pregnancy were terminated, of injury to the physical or mental health of the pregnant woman or any existing children of the family; or

- that the termination is necessary to prevent grave permanent injury to the physical or mental health of the pregnant woman; or

- that the continuance of the pregnancy would involve risk to the life of the pregnant woman, greater than if the pregnancy were terminated; or

- that there is a substantial risk that if the child were born it would suffer from physical or mental abnormalities as to be seriously handicapped'.[1]

Although we will discuss a professional's right to conscientious objection to abortion in Chapter 11, essentially if someone has a conscientious objection they are not under a legal duty to participate in an abortion. As we shall see, the situation of a healthcare chaplain is not clear. However, in a medical

---

1   Department of Health (1967) Abortion Act. London: HMSO, section 1

emergency, conscientious objection is not a defence, though the doctor can call on another colleague. The Act does not remove the duty to advise, so the doctor must still refer the patient to a colleague. The doctor still owes duties to patients post-abortion.

Given that a foetus at 24 weeks has more protection than a foetus at 20 weeks, the law takes a gradual approach to the moral status of the developing human being. Some people argue that it is discriminatory for the law to allow for abortion up to term for a foetus with a substantial risk of serious disability, particularly since there is no legal definition of 'substantial' or 'serious' and disability is often interpreted very broadly.

Little research has been conducted into the psychological effects of termination on women. However, if a woman has been unduly influenced or felt pressurised or lacked support then the psychological effects may be greater.

Case study: ethical implications

See: In many cases, there are pressures put on people that make it difficult for them to see clearly. Moreover, it is often difficult to find hope, to see alternatives or to persevere in times of crisis. Since the chaplain stands outside the situation, the chaplain can give a different perspective and offer that hope. In acting ethically, the chaplain should see according to his conscience, and a proper formation of conscience includes knowing the stand his faith tradition takes on the issue of abortion. The chaplain should also see that not everyone he ministers to is aware of or adheres to their own faith tradition. This may be a result of a failure to understand, or of cultural blindness or an unwillingness to find out. In order to grasp the reality of the concrete situation, these are some of the realities that the chaplain needs to ascertain. Has not an unborn baby already come into the world?

Judge: Is there enough information? How many people are you ministering to? Would you include the unborn babies? If you choose to act in a particular way, will that action compromise your position as a representative of a particular faith? And your personal integrity?

Act: Active and attentive listening is a priority. Do you need to seek advice? Can you support the person's spiritual needs?

Some further comments

It is hardly surprising that a pregnant woman who discovers that there may be a problem with her baby is in emotional turmoil. What should be a happy time becomes a time of great uncertainty and anxiety. Blame, fear, grief and loss of an anticipated 'perfect' future may contribute to feelings of confusion and loneliness, and it is more difficult if people do not feel that they have the support of their family. The mere fact that someone else can *see* that this is a confusing time will help when it comes to clarifying issues.

Whether or not Alison goes for further diagnostic tests, she may be faced with a decision to continue the pregnancy or end the pregnancy with a termination. When confronted with such a decision, many women are in complete shock and feel that their whole world has collapsed and all their hopes for the future have been dashed. Some women simply cannot see a way forward, time seems to stand still and they exist as if in a fog of emotions. The option to continue with the pregnancy seems fraught with difficulty, worries about coping, and anxiety over the suffering of the baby, especially where family support is lacking, and for many women the option to terminate the pregnancy becomes extremely painful and distressing. The chaplain *acts* in a valuable role by helping Alison take time and find the inner space to listen to and evaluate the many competing voices she may be hearing.

While Alison may be facing a situation where her baby might be born with a disability, Bill and Caroline have been told it is likely that their baby will be stillborn or die soon after birth.

Many couples are very concerned that their baby will suffer, and so they are inclined to opt for a termination out of compassion. Some couples may think that their baby is doomed anyway, and others may feel that they cannot themselves emotionally survive the remaining weeks until birth. Active listening allows people to voice all their fears in a way that accompanies rather than shuts down. The chaplain can also challenge some negative and discriminatory attitudes towards a life of disability.

The situations of Alison and Bill and Caroline are similar in many ways, so what is said about the support that the chaplain can offer applies in both situations, although for simplicity's sake we will discuss these in relation to Bill and Caroline.

First, the chaplain can give them time and suggest that they take time. Taking a deep breath and standing back will help Bill and Caroline to begin to take in the information and at least partially recover from the initial shock. Taking time to understand the medical information and the possible condition of the baby will help them think through the alternatives. In the safe space of their encounter the chaplain can encourage them to name their fears, to talk about their views on termination and the challenges of disability. This is particularly important if Bill and Caroline are to make a joint decision. In the ethics of communication it is necessary to hear all those who wish to be heard. The couple may also be encouraged to think about how they will feel about their choice in a few years' time after this crisis has passed.

Second, the chaplain can remind Bill and Caroline that they can have ongoing spiritual support. Many couples fear that they will be left alone in their decision-making or will be abandoned to their grief and loss. The ongoing support is different from routine pregnancy support in the sense that the support is shaped by the profound reality of grief that accompanies the pregnancy and the reality of the care that will be given when the baby is born and after the baby dies. The chaplain can remind Bill and Caroline that continuing the pregnancy is not about doing nothing or passively waiting for the baby to die. It is about actively loving and embracing this little life, however short it is.

Chaplains who are appointed as representatives of their faith community should remain in good standing with that faith tradition. Therefore, it is crucial that the chaplain knows what the faith tradition has to say on key issues such as abortion, following conscience, freedom, responsibility and discipleship. The chaplain will then be able to minister effectively, with pastoral sensitivity and with hope to someone who comes from the same faith tradition. The chaplain remembers that there are three people involved here – Bill, Caroline and their unborn baby – and a gentle reminder to a mother that her unborn child is loved just for who he or she is and will always be held in the palm of God's hand whatever happens may offer some comfort. Often women think that they simply have no choice but to opt for a termination, especially if they think that the baby will suffer. In the long term, a woman who feels pressurised into a termination may still find it difficult to come to terms with what she has done and she may even blame herself for not being stronger. It is important for the chaplain to open up the possibilities for responsible choice, notably the possibilities in perinatal and palliative care. Once again, giving time and space and the opportunity of naming the baby, of baptism if the baby lives even a short while, and ritual to mark the baby's existence and later the ritual of the funeral arrangements can help to lead the person through the darkness. Much work has been done on the healing nature of giving parents the opportunity to hold their baby even after the baby has died, on creating memory boxes and on helping new parents face bereavement.

A response to difficulties in pregnancy should take into account support for those who choose not to have a termination as well as compassion and appropriate forgiveness for those who do have terminations. Many women will go on to suffer depression and the equivalent of post-traumatic stress, especially when they have had doubts about their course of action. **Prayer to find the right words and act with compassion is pivotal.**

Observing and respecting spoken and unspoken feelings is crucial. Engaging with the mother, partner and family where they are at and not merely where you think they should be is vital. Giving adequate time is essential. Remember the parents not only in your prayers but also in the months to come and follow up where possible. You need to be aware of the emotional toll on yourself, especially when decisions are difficult and the outcome is not what you had hoped for.

REFLECTION

Is there a difference between supporting someone before they have an abortion or after they have made that decision and plan to go ahead with an abortion, or after they have had an abortion? What difference does disability make? Why?

Summary

In reflecting on the situation of an unborn baby with possible disability we have looked at perhaps one of the more challenging aspects of the beginning of life. This may have taken away from various claims about the termination of pregnancy. Some people claim that reproductive ethics and in particular the question of termination are purely private affairs and that the conditions of the Abortion Act restrict the freedom of women to make their own life decisions. Some people argue that the UK has moved from abortion as an option in extreme cases as a matter of compassion, through abortion as an option on request grounded in female liberation and the right to choose, to a duty to abort, a duty put forward by those who argue that it is irresponsible to bring to birth a child with disabilities. What do you think?

Our next chapter deals with ethical issues concerning babies and young children.

Chapter 7

ETHICAL ISSUES ABOUT BABIES, CHILDREN AND YOUNG ADULTS

CASE STUDY

The chaplain has just been to visit baby George who was born at 39 weeks and has been diagnosed with a condition with possibly life-threatening medical complications that will inevitably lead to significant developmental delay. George's parents have heard the nurses talking among themselves about palliative care as the best option and they are beginning to think that the medical profession is giving up on their son. George's parents, who are very religious, want their son to have everything done for him, because they believe that life is sacred to God. To George's parents, it seems that the whole discussion is about whether George should live or die.

Meanwhile, Harry has popped in to see a member of the chaplaincy team, while his parents are speaking to the doctor. Harry is now 16. He explains that when he was eight, he was diagnosed with cancer, so he knows all about the effects of treatment, and it seems that the cancer has now returned. Harry says he has asked the doctor what the treatment would involve this time and the doctor has told him that the treatment will have side effects that are different for everyone, but that the therapy works. Harry knew that his parents wanted to speak with the doctor so he left them to it even though Harry had already told his parents that he wanted to make up his own mind about treatment. Harry is worried that the doctor and his parents may be keeping him in the dark about the possible side effects, and Harry has looked online and reckons that aggressive treatment may leave him unable to have children. He feels embarrassed to talk about this with his parents, because he knows they are really worried that he may not make it through the cancer this time without treatment.

At the end of the day, Isabel, a radiologist new to the hospital, steps into the chaplaincy office to ask for advice. When she was taking an x-ray for a suspected arm fracture of a toddler, she had noticed two other healed fractures. Isabel is concerned but does not want to make a fuss in case this is not really evidence of abuse.

REFLECTION

What principles are significant when considering who decides for children and young people? Autonomy? Capacity? Who has responsibility? What about the sanctity of life?

What are your priorities for the day?

Decisions and children

The person-centred approach to ethical concerns in healthcare involves the relationship between the patient and the healthcare chaplain. However, where a child or young person is concerned, the situation becomes more complex, since the patient's world usually but not always includes parents and siblings, people who are important to the child and who also have a legitimate interest in how the child is cared for. Certainly, it is true that we all live in a network of relationships; we are, after all, social beings. But there can be obvious tensions when the child's voice, or what others presume is the child's best interests, is in conflict with the voice or wishes of parents. Do we accept the child's voice? Do we simply assume that the child's best interests are served by respecting parental wishes and so maintaining family unity? Does the doctor know best? Does the age of the child matter? Or is it a case of maturity?

The child's welfare, the child's voice and family unity are all relevant considerations. Parents have the primary responsibility for their children and generally they are best placed to know and understand the unique needs of their child and to make appropriate caring decisions. Doctors have a duty to provide the standard of care that meets the patient's needs and to minimise harm. Many cases of conflict arise because the communication between all the people involved breaks down and people begin to suspect each other's motives. The stress and distress that parents understandably feel may cause them to feel that undue external influence is pressurising them into making certain decisions. Parents may feel uncertain and even hostile about the treatment goals of doctors and may think that the medical profession is simply giving up on their child. Doctors may think that parents are being unrealistic or even in denial about their child's situation and so categorise them as difficult to deal with and troublesome. In their zeal to minimise harm, doctors may refuse to tolerate any harm at all and so will simply decide on an intervention without considering a different intervention that would be more acceptable to the parent's.

Although some people think of parental decision-making in terms of the right of parents to make choices, it may be helpful to think of parental decision-making in terms of the responsibility parents have in supporting the interests of their child and in fostering family unity. A shift in the conversation away from rights and what the parents want to responsibility may contribute to creating dialogue.

However, there may also be conflict between parents. Often this may come out of earlier unresolved issues, or it may be that the parents have a different understanding about what is in their child's best interests.

The healthcare chaplain once again occupies a unique space between parents, children and doctors, where good communication and negotiation can take place. The chaplain does not make clinical decisions or control how people interact. This neutrality allows the chaplain to listen to and advocate on behalf of parents who may feel disempowered by the professionals as well as to explain and reflect on proposed decisions. It also allows the chaplain to listen to and feedback on the views of the child or young person, obviously with consent of the young person where appropriate. Neutrality also enables the chaplain to bring to the fore other considerations apart from autonomy and enabling choice. By offering a broader perspective and including elements such as good stewardship, cherishing life as well as recognising the limits of life, the chaplain can open up a deeper context for decision-making.

Information: treating young people

As a general principle, in an emergency, treatment can be given to a child or young person without consent if the aim of the treatment is to save the child's life or prevent serious deterioration of the child's health. The question of who consents to treatment in non-emergency situations depends in part on the young person's age and their capacity. As a general rule, even when children are not old enough to make their own decisions, they should be involved as far as possible in decisions about their care.

When a person becomes 18, no one can consent on their behalf, and if the person does not have capacity to make a decision, then the principles of the Mental Capacity Act 2005 apply and a decision is made taking account of their best interests. There is something of a grey area in the law when it comes to young people who are between 16 and 17. There is a general presumption that young people over 16 have the capacity to consent to treatment unless evidence suggests otherwise, and an assessment of their capacity to consent follows the same principles for capacity in the Mental Capacity Act. However, if treatment for a young person under 18 has been agreed by a person with parental responsibility or by the courts, and treatment is in the young person's best interests, any refusal of treatment by the young person can be overriden.

Young people of this age, then, do not have the same rights as adults since they cannot refuse treatment that is in their best interests. However, they can consent to treatment, although it is recommended as part of good practice that any decision does involve someone with parental responsibility. This is unless it is considered not to be in the young person's interests to involve a parent. If a young person has capacity for a decision and they ask for their confidentiality to be kept, then chaplains and doctors should respect this wish, unless failing to disclose information is considered to result in significant harm to the young person. It is prudent for the chaplain to explain to a young person that the chaplain may not be able to promise to keep what is said confidential if what is disclosed suggests that the young person may be at risk.

It cannot be assumed that just because a young person has learning difficulties they lack capacity – giving the person the appropriate amount and level of information in an appropriate manner can help them to be involved in decision-making. If a child is under 18 but not considered to have capacity, then someone with parental responsibility can give consent. Usually it is only necessary to ask one person with parental responsibility to consent, but it is good practice to include anyone who is significant to the child.

The Children Act 1989 explains who has parental responsibility.[1] A mother always has parental responsibility for her child, and a father has responsibility only if he was married to the child's mother when the child was born. A father can also acquire responsibility if he jointly registered the birth of the child with the mother or if he has a parental responsibility agreement with the mother or if the court has made a parental responsibility order. If a child has a legally appointed guardian or the court has made a residence order for the child, then that person also has parental responsibility. A local authority may

---

1 The Children Act 1989 applies to England and Wales; for Scotland see the Children (Scotland) Act 1995; for Northern Ireland see the Children (Northern Ireland) Order 1995

have responsibility if a care order or protection order has been made concerning the child. If the parents themselves are under 16, they may not have parental responsibility. Foster parents and grandparents do not automatically have parental responsibility.

A person with parental responsibility has the right to consent to treatment on behalf of a child if the child cannot consent. However, treatment must always be in the interests of the child. If parents do not agree and this disagreement cannot be resolved informally, then the person seeking consent may apply to the courts. This also applies where doctors do not think that a decision by a parent is in the best interests of the child. The person with parental responsibility can also access their child's health records, but if the young person is deemed capable of giving consent then their consent must be given.

Gillick competency test and Fraser guidelines

For children under 16, capacity to consent to treatment without involvement of parents is governed by the Gillick competency test. The Gillick competency test was named after a 1983 case brought by a mother, Mrs Gillick, who sought to challenge healthcare guidance that would have allowed her daughters under the age of 16 to receive confidential contraceptive advice without her consent. Lord Fraser was one of the law lords involved in the case, and his judgement referring specifically to contraceptive or sexual health advice and treatment has now become the Fraser guidelines. The Fraser guidelines have been further extended to include termination of pregnancy. The Gillick competency test is broader than the Fraser guidelines, because it applies to competency for children under 16 to consent to any treatment. There is no lower age limit for Gillick competence.

Under the Gillick competency test, a child under 16 can consent to treatment if they have sufficient understanding and intelligence to take on board fully what the proposed treatment involves. This includes appreciating the purpose, nature, effects and risks of the intended treatment as well as the chances of success and the availability of other options. If the child passes this test, the child is Gillick competent to consent. However, the child's consent must be voluntarily given, and they must not be subject to any undue influence. The child's competency must be tested each time for different decisions, since the understanding of different treatments may vary. If the child does not pass the test, then treatment can proceed with the consent of a person with parental responsibility or by court order.

Safeguarding

Child abuse can take many forms – it can be physical, emotional, sexual or involve neglect. Child protection from abuse is everyone's responsibility. Following the Children Act 1989 the welfare of the child is paramount, and since the best place for a child to be brought up and cared for is within their own family as far as is possible, agencies should work in partnership with families. Of course, this applies as long as this does not prejudice the welfare of the child. A child who is in danger should be protected and be kept safe by prompt and effective action. The child should be told about what is happening, should be listened to and should participate as far as possible in any decisions about their future.

Following the Children Act 2004, agencies must work together in safeguarding and promoting the welfare of children. In the NHS there are designated people who take a strategic lead in safeguarding, and they are usually the principal point of contact for anyone who has any concerns about a child. They also organise and run training sessions for members of staff.

There is other legislation that is relevant to children. In 1991, the UK ratified the United Nations Convention on the Rights of the Child and under this convention any decision or action concerning children should be focused on their best interests. In connection with children and their families, the Human Rights Act 1998 has enshrined the right to life (Article 2), the prohibition of torture, inhuman or degrading treatment or punishment (Article 3), the right to a fair trial (Article 6) and respect for private and family life (Article 8). The UK government document published in 2015, *What to do if you are worried a child is being abused,* gives guidelines to help all professionals respond appropriately to safeguarding concerns. You can find a link to this in the Resources section.

If a child wants to confide in you as a chaplain, you have to tread very carefully. Any questioning of the child may be interpreted as asking leading questions, and this may affect later police investigations. You should listen carefully and record verbatim the whole discussion as soon as possible. Observe how the child is and record this as well. Try not to make any assumptions or interpret what the child is saying. You should not promise to keep what the child says confidential and explain why gently and carefully. Your written record should show timings, be dated, signed and witnessed, and you should contact a senior member of the chaplaincy team and the person designated on the child protection team.

Case study: ethical implications

See: Sometimes it is difficult to get a good grasp of the situation if you only hear one side of the story. Have you visited baby George? Have you spoken to the healthcare team? Have the parents really heard and understood what the nurses said? Part of seeing is also finding out more about the religious beliefs of the parents. Are there different ways of interpreting that life is sacred to God? Seeing also involves grasping what a person wants from their encounter with the chaplain. Does Harry want someone to talk to simply about making a decision or about his life and possible dying? Would he welcome the intervention of a chaplain or should the chaplain think in terms of empowering Harry?

Judge: While it is important to know lines of responsibility for decision-making, ethical concern also includes creating or restoring as far as possible lines of communication, so that those decisions can be made with proper regard to all those involved. Issues of safeguarding require prompt and careful judgement and you should know the safeguarding policy of your institution. While safeguarding is everyone's responsibility, does this line of responsibility begin with Isabel or the chaplain?

Act: And the spiritual welfare of baby George? If this has not been done, is it appropriate to discuss baptism or a blessing of the baby? Do you know when and if a ritual of anointing applies in your faith tradition? Does the action of the chaplain depend on what Harry wants? And a prudent application of safeguarding?

Some further comments

In the case of baby George, it is important to *see* how the communication is between the parents and the healthcare team, as it seems that there could be a rapid slide into a breakdown in communication between the medical staff and George's parents. It is not at all clear what the team has said among themselves, or whether this does in fact have real implications for the treatment of baby George. While parents do have the first responsibility for their child, the child's treatment should be appropriate and in his best interests. It is important that staff explain clearly and with careful understanding what they think is the appropriate treatment, and if it is thought that palliative care is the best option, this should also be justified before any final decision is taken so that the views of the parents can be taken into account. Keeping everyone informed and in the conversation is crucial to maintain trust and to enable reaching a wise decision. As a faith representative, the chaplain is well placed to *act* by clarifying religious beliefs and helping fellow believers reflect on their particular faith tradition. Where communication shows signs of breaking down, the chaplain can be a helpful negotiator and also an advocate in the process. The healthcare team may not be aware of the significance of religious beliefs for the family, and a discussion with the chaplain may help the team to see that this is not simply an issue of privately held ideas or false hopes.

If you have been asked to baptise a baby on a ward, you must keep to infection control standards. This includes using sterilised water that you can then bless, and an aluminium dish. Remember to fill out the baptismal certificate and baptism details form and enter the details into the hospital register. Sometimes when the baby is in an incubator, it may be difficult to reach the baby's head, so you can soak some cotton wool in water and drop some water onto, for instance the baby's hand.

It is difficult to *judge* or gauge the maturity and level of understanding of some young people, but someone like Harry who is 16 should be involved as far as possible with decisions regarding his treatment. Although Harry has had cancer treatment before, it cannot simply be assumed that he is aware of the effects of treatment. Nevertheless, his experience should be taken into account, and his concerns should be treated seriously. Many parents do find it difficult to let go of their children and allow them to make decisions, especially when the stakes are so high. Once again, opening up a space for communication is important here. But if Harry has come to the chaplain in confidence, then that confidence is to be respected. If Harry's parents and doctors decide that treatment is necessary, then treatment may be given. However, if Harry wants the chaplain to be a part of the conversation, the chaplain should think about how to facilitate a productive discussion, pointing out perhaps that if Harry does not think he has been given full information or is being kept out of the conversation, he may feel betrayed and his trust in the healthcare system may be dented. He may then refuse treatment when he becomes an adult. Moreover, a patient who understands and agrees to a care plan is much more likely to follow it through.

The healthcare situations of baby George and his parents, and Harry and his parents are likely to last for some time. The chaplain should make sure that if the families want it she has follow-up meetings and regularly assesses the spiritual needs of all those involved as the circumstances are likely to change. The chaplain should be prepared to *see*, so that she understands as the situations of baby George and Harry change and develop, to *judge* what else is required and to *act*, so that the families can be better prepared for what lies ahead.

When it comes to suspected child abuse, people are naturally worried that if they report a suspicion and they turn out to be wrong, then this could have grave consequences for the family. Similarly, if they do not report a suspicion, the child may suffer further injury or possibly even death. However, research shows that a significant minority of children in the UK do suffer from serious abuse. Often it is professionals such as the radiographer who first come across potential instances of abuse, and so as a matter of course, they must be vigilant and remember that the child's safety is their first concern. As a radiologist, Isabel is not the primary healthcare professional for the toddler, and so she may not know other medical information relevant to the toddler's care, such as congenital rickets which may be the cause of multiple fractures. Nevertheless, she still has a responsibility towards the child; everyone involved in healthcare should be a 'safeguarder'. No single professional can have a full picture of all of a child's circumstances and needs, so sharing information and identifying concerns can ensure that the child gets the right help. The priority is to address the safety and welfare of the child while also remembering that the child is in a family.

All healthcare professionals should know and follow the procedures provided by their organisation or institution. Isabel should immediately discuss any concerns initially with a senior member of staff. She should make a detailed record of her observations and action taken, and she should date this, have it witnessed and kept in a safe place. She should also contact the designated professional or appropriate person named in her institution's safeguarding policy and give them a copy of her record of concern. The chaplain should also speak to her own line manager, make a note of any actions, make any referrals in writing and record the outcome of each referral. It is wise not to assume that other healthcare professionals have reported their concerns already. It is not the role of either Isabel or the chaplain to inform parents or to investigate further. However, Isabel and the chaplain can expect to have some feedback from the child protection team.

REFLECTION

In the case study, how useful is it to describe the situation of George in terms of whether the baby should live or die? Can you find a better description?

Is it easy to make unwarranted assumptions based on age? Or religious belief? Or initial appearances?

Miscarriage and stillbirth

If there are worries about an unborn baby, an ultrasound scan can check the baby's heartbeat. In some cases the baby may have died. Parents are usually given time to think about what to do next, and as long as there is no danger to the mother's health, the mother may decide to wait for labour to begin naturally, or she may ask for the baby to be induced. If the baby has died before 24 weeks of pregnancy, then the mother has had a miscarriage. A stillborn birth happens when a baby is born with no signs of life after 24 weeks of pregnancy. In England and Wales, the birth of a stillborn baby has to be formally registered. Understandably, the tragedy of miscarriage and stillbirth is devastating and how parents cope is very personal. When a baby is stillborn, some parents do not want to see their baby, others want to be able to see the baby and hold him or her. Many parents want to give the baby a name, to have him or her blessed and to take photographs.

For the chaplain, as for any other member of staff, the untimely death of a baby can be very difficult. Prayer with the family, reminding them that however short the baby's life, the baby was loved by them and is loved by God, can help with the healing. Observation may reveal that although work in the neonatal unit has its rewards, it can also have great emotional impact on nurses. Often professionals feel helpless because there are some things that cannot be fixed and dealing with the utter heartbreak of a family can be emotionally draining. Healthcare staff have spiritual needs as well. Engaging with parents who feel either nothing because they are numb with shock or who feel everything calls for sensitivity. Time as always is essential. Remembering for some parents becomes a crucial way of coping, and many chaplaincy teams have put in place religious memorial services or special days when parents who have suffered loss can come together to remember their children. In particular, many people mourn silently the loss of a baby through miscarriage because more often than not there was no baby to see. You also have to remember your own need to debrief and recharge your spiritual batteries.

Summary

We have seen that the ethical issues concerning babies, children and young adults go beyond autonomy and decision-making. These issues reach into the heart of families and relationships as well as relationships with healthcare professionals. Perhaps this is a salutary reminder that all of us, children and adults, live in a network of relationships.

Much of our discussion has involved, at least implicitly, talk of dying and the end of life. In our next chapter we turn to the end of life and ask, when do I die?

Chapter 8

ETHICAL ISSUES AT THE END OF LIFE

CASE STUDY

The chaplain has been called to support Mr and Mrs Kelly, the parents of 26-year-old Liam. A few weeks ago, Liam was in a car accident. He has not been declared brain dead, but he has not regained consciousness and his doctors think he may be in a vegetative state. This can only be confirmed after observation over some time, once Liam has been taken off ventilation, and if he breathes on his own. Mr and Mrs Kelly think that their son's injuries are so catastrophic that all treatment should be stopped, he should be taken off ventilation and that if he is in a permanent vegetative state all treatment should be withdrawn. It seems that unknown to Mr and Mrs Kelly, Liam had been carrying a donor card. The medical team inform the transplant team, and it is suggested that Liam be kept on the ventilator. Mr and Mrs Kelly are distraught, since they do not know when they will be able to say goodbye properly to their son, and they do not like the thought of Liam suffering further. Moreover, they do not know if their faith allows organ donation.

The chaplain has promised to visit Joan, an elderly lady he knows well. When he arrives on the ward, he finds Joan's daughter Kim and Joan's son Mike arguing. Their mother can no longer speak and is drifting in and out of consciousness. The nurse thinks that Joan does not have much time left. Although the chaplain and the nurse try and calm the situation, Kim and Mike continue to argue, with Kim complaining that she has done all the care for their mother and Mike protesting that Kim always has to act the martyr. The chaplain holds Joan's hand and asks her if she wants to be anointed. Joan squeezes his hand.

> ### REFLECTION
> Can there be a warm, breathing, heart-beating dead body? Do we always remember that the patient is not yet dead?

When am I dead?

In healthcare settings, it is a simple fact that patients do die, and it has long been recognised that the dead should be treated with a high level of respect. However, we may want to ask what criteria should be followed in order to declare someone dead? This kind of question is not simply a matter of whether or not we all agree on the criteria, nor is it about whether the criteria are safe. Our idea of death comes out of what we mean when we speak about a living human person. To grasp this, it may help if we ask ourselves the question: is it always obvious when someone is alive or dead? If we took a list of different states that people are in between being alive and being dead, then the answer to this question is generally obvious. If I am awake, I am alive; if I am asleep, I am alive; if I am not breathing on my own, my heart is no longer beating, no blood is circulating, my brain has ceased all activity and there has been a total system collapse, then I am dead. But what about some intermediate stages? What about when someone has locked-in syndrome – this is when the person is conscious and aware, but they are completely paralysed, though they may be able to communicate by blinking or eye gazing? The person in this situation is still alive. What about a patient in a coma – the patient shows no signs of being awake or of being aware and they do not respond to their environment? Again it seems that the patient is alive. While the comatose patient may wake up and recover, they may instead progress to a vegetative state. In this case, the patient has wake and sleep cycles, breathes on their own and may cough, blink and make noises. However, it seems that there are no signs of meaningful responses. A patient in a vegetative state may enter a minimally conscious state if they show evidence of minimal but inconsistent awareness. If there is no change in vegetative state after several months to a year, the patient may be judged to be in a permanent vegetative state, where recovery is extremely unlikely but not impossible.

Notice the language used here: vegetative may suggest to some people that there is no *personal* or *human* life here, even if the body is alive. Indeed, comments in the court case of Tony Bland, a young man who suffered catastrophic brain damage in the Hillsborough disaster in 1989 that left him in a permanent vegetative state, expressed precisely this view. Supported by his family, Tony Bland's health authority asked the courts to rule if it could lawfully discontinue treatment including the administration of food and fluids. In court, one judge said that Tony Bland was alive, but his existence in a permanent vegetative state was a 'living death', another declared that, to all intents and purposes Tony Bland was 'dead'. His spirit has left him, and all that remained was the shell of his body'.[1]

From both a religious and non-religious point of view it does seem problematic to refer to some living human beings as vegetables or empty shells or alive but without a life. However, some faith traditions are also cautious about determining the exact moment of death. In part, this reflects a belief in the mystery of both death and life; it honours the person whose life is coming to an end and it leaves space for life beyond death. In some traditions such as Hinduism and Buddhism, the cessation of the functions of the body is the beginning of the dying process, not its end. In some traditions, any breath signifies life even if that breath is maintained mechanically. In other traditions, death is defined as when the soul or the life force leaves the body or when the life faculty is extinguished.

---

1   Lord Goff, p.366, Lord Brown, p.833, *Airedale NHS Trust v Bland* (1993)

Since these moments are not visible, empirical evidence is then used to determine that death has in fact taken place. This caution is reflected in rituals of prayer, chanting, leaving the patient undisturbed for some hours after death and handling the body. For many people, the human being, alive and dead, belongs to God and so the body can never be regarded merely as raw material. This means that how the body is treated after death remains ethically significant.

There is no doubt that organ donation is a heroic act of love and it gives life to other human beings. However, we may wish to think harder about the ethical basis for donation. In a system where everyone is automatically a donor, unless they choose not to be, it would seem that the state more or less owns a person's body, or at least parts of it, since it is the state that decides what is to be done with the body after death. In a system where each person chooses whether or not to be a donor and what to donate then the focus is on the charitable act of giving of the person. Moreover, good stewardship of our bodies requires that we cherish the life we have while accepting death. We cannot deliberately hasten death and we have to be careful about when we declare a person dead.

It is clear then that there are particular ethical concerns regarding the donation of vital organs, that is organs that are not paired such as the heart and are vital for the continuing existence of a person. Some of these ethical concerns include who decides about organ donation and on what basis, and does the donor of a vital organ have to be dead, in which case how do we define death?

So, when are you dead?

Information
Defining death
Historically in the UK, the absence of heartbeat and breathing, so the cessation of heart and lung function, signalled death. Without oxygenated blood the body cannot survive. With the

possibility of interventions that help with ventilation and circulation, heart and lung functions can be maintained artificially, and these functions became replaceable. Moreover, the heart can now be bypassed or replaced, and this indicates that some organs are not constitutive of the person – my heart can die without me dying. In the USA in 1968, a new criterion for defining death was suggested: brain death. In the UK, not loss of all brain function but death of the brain stem which leads to the irreversible loss of the capacity for consciousness combined with irreversible loss of the capacity to breathe spontaneously is regarded as one of the definitions of death. Determining brain stem death requires specific and lengthy medical tests that take place over 24 hours. Another definition of death is the cessation of breathing and absence of heartbeat.

At the same time as the brain death criteria were being formulated, organ donation procedures were being perfected. In the UK there are different types of organ donation. Donation of a single kidney, blood, bone marrow or a piece of liver can be from a living donor. Tissue can be donated from a living or, in some cases, a dead donor. However, for vital organs such as the liver, kidney, heart and lungs the UK follows the 'dead donor rule': donation can be done only after the donor has been declared dead, and currently death is determined either following the brain death criteria or death following the cessation of the circulatory system. Implicit in organ donation is a rule of consent so that the usual standards of medical care are not compromised.

Given the very many people waiting for organ transplants, the positive attitude towards organ donation in intensive care settings and the fact that some families have suggested organ donation from their relatives who were not brain dead, there has been a rise in the number of cases of death diagnosed by the circulatory cardiac criteria. Organ donation can then take place either after an unexpected cardiac arrest in a critically ill patient or in a controlled manner when cardiac arrest is expected.

With controlled cardiac arrest the patient who has suffered an overwhelming organ failure, often of the brain, is usually on ventilation. If it has been decided that it is in the patient's best interests to withdraw treatment and it is expected that circulation would cease within three hours on withdrawal of the life-sustaining treatment, then there may be discussions about organ donation. During these discussions consent must be checked or obtained from the family by a specialist nurse for organ donation (SNOD). Withdrawal of treatment takes place only when the surgical retrieval team is ready and the recipients of the organs have been identified and so it can be some time after consent has been given.

Consent

The law about consent and organ donation varies across the UK. The Human Tissue Act 2004 states that organ donation can only proceed if consent has been provided by either the donor, or someone nominated by the donor or by the donor's family. Under the 'opt in' system, if a patient has already recorded their wish to donate their organs on the organ donation register then this consent to donation should normally be respected. In Wales, there is an 'opt out' system whereby consent to donate is presumed; a person has to opt out of the system if she does not want to donate her organs.

Where there is no record of wishes

If a patient is unconscious or unable to make decisions and has not recorded their wishes on the organ donation register and the family do not offer any evidence either way of the family member's intentions, then medical staff can ask the relatives for a decision. If no family or friends can be contacted, then donation will not proceed, because there has not been consent and, in terms of safety, there is no medical and social history of the patient.

The family members are usually approached by the SNOD who tries first to establish whether the patient had expressed any wishes regarding donation. If there is no evidence either way then the SNOD determines which of the family members is best placed to give a decision based on the hierarchy of relationships within the family as set out in the Human Tissue Act 2004.[2] First in this hierarchy is a spouse or partner, then a parent or child, then brother or sister, then grandparent or grandchild, then nephew or niece, then step-father or step-mother, followed by half-sibling and then a long-standing friend. The aim of the discussion with the family is to support an informed decision, not to persuade to donate. Where there is disagreement among family members, the person at the top of the hierarchy has the final say. However, the SNOD and other healthcare staff should help the family reach a consensus. Clearly there is an important role here for the chaplain who can be particularly attentive to the concerns of different people, and notably where these concerns stem from religious worries.

The SNOD gives a description of what is involved in the donation process, especially where there is withdrawal of treatment. The SNOD also explains the procedure relevant either to donation after brain stem death or donation after circulatory death. The discussion includes interventions that may take place before or after death. The family may also be asked to consent to tissue donation, blood tests from the patient, and research. As part of the procedure for informed decision-making, the SNOD asks the family about the patient's recent medical and social history. Sometimes the family simply do not want to answer social or health questions about the patient and in this case the SNOD tells the family that the patient will be regarded as a 'higher-risk donor'.

At the time of publication in England, if a patient has previously refused to donate their organs then this cannot be overruled by the family. In Wales a patient has to opt out.

---

2   In Scotland this is the Human Tissue (Scotland) Act 2006

Where the patient is on the organ donation register

Even when the patient has previously registered a wish to donate their organs, the SNOD still approaches the family to discuss what will happen, though this time the SNOD can assume that the family will give support to the patient's wishes. It is helpful if the SNOD has a hard copy of the organ donation register or the patient's organ donation card to confirm the patient's consent. Legally the patient's previously recorded consent is sufficient for donation to go ahead. However, there are situations where the family may not agree. The family may argue that the patient no longer wanted to donate organs, and they must provide evidence of why that may be. Evidence that the patient's wishes have changed is not overruling the consent of the patient. Rather, it is presenting new evidence that challenges that original consent. The family may disagree among themselves about whether or not the patient wanted to donate, and in this case the SNOD may have to weigh up all the competing claims, although where the patient has formally registered, there is a presumption in favour of donation. The family may accept that the patient did want to donate, but they may say that the specific context of this donation means that they do not want to proceed with the donation. For instance, if it is proposed that the donation process will take a prolonged amount of time or require invasive procedures, then the context in which the patient originally consented may appear to have changed. This calls for the SNOD to reassess what is in the patient's best interests.

Interventions before and after death

Some interventions before and after death are done in order to optimise donor organ quality and improve the outcome of the transplant. This means that a patient may be declared brain dead, and then if their heart stops, cardiopulmonary resuscitation (CPR) may be used to keep the heart beating and ensure organs remain oxygenated. In the case of donation after cardiac arrest, preparation happens before the patient is dead, and the patient is taken to theatre for surgery while still alive. In all of these situations it is often very difficult for families to accept that their loved ones have died.

Case study: ethical implications

See: In attempting to grasp complex situations it may be useful to separate out some of the elements. It may take time for some people to come to terms with the outcome of an accident, and how people are coping may be reflected in what they do and say. Members of the family of an accident victim may also be concerned about coping with the idea that their loved one may be profoundly and permanently disabled. How can the chaplain help them face what is a new reality? In a great many cases, doctors cannot be precise in their prognosis and a family may find it too difficult to deal with uncertainty. In addition, there is the surprise of organ donation, and this may be especially hard to work through when the people concerned do not agree or are not sure if organ donation conflicts with their religious beliefs. The prospect of having come to terms with the imminent dying of a loved one, and then discovering that the person's life will be prolonged for some time with no apparent benefit for that person can be very distressing. It may be helpful for Mr and Mrs Kelly to have a clearer understanding of the process so that they know what to expect should donation go ahead. Are not the spiritual needs of Liam a central question for the chaplain – after all, Liam is not dead? Does the same apply to Joan?

Judge: Who decides whether the treatment is stopped or continued in preparation for donation? Can death be in a patient's best interests? The chaplain may wish to see the conversation around donation as part of the bereavement process for Mr and Mrs Kelly. Do you know where your faith tradition stands on the issue of organ donation? How does this fit in with concern for Liam's spiritual needs? In situations where there are multiple needs, the chaplain must judge his priorities: does administering last rites trump everything?

Act: Prayers, ritual and the sacraments for Liam and Joan are significant aspects of care here. Perhaps you could remind yourself of the 'dead donor rule'.

Some further comments

In cases such as Liam's, family distress is clearly to be expected, and many people find it difficult to take in all that is happening, especially where there are so many uncertainties. Although the chaplain has been called to minister to Mr and Mrs Kelly, the chaplain would do well to *see* clearly and remember that the patient is still a patient, and a decision to withdraw treatment should be made on ethically acceptable grounds with this patient in mind (see Chapter 9) and not linked to the proposed organ donation. Moreover, the chaplain may wish to ask about the spiritual needs of Liam, and in particular if Liam's parents think that he would like to receive any prayers, ritual or sacraments.

A further difficulty is that the outcome for Liam is not at all clear. He may not be dying. Whether Liam can breathe on his own or not will only be known once he is taken off the ventilator. If he does breathe on his own, it may be sometime before the doctors decide that he is in a permanent vegetative state. Liam's parents may have to think about their son as being profoundly disabled, but this is not the same as being as good as dead. If they are certain that they want all treatment to be withdrawn, then they must also think about whether or not their son should receive food and fluids, since under English law this is also treatment.

Mr and Mrs Kelly suggest that they do not know if their faith tradition accepts organ donation. As a chaplain, you should be ready to answer on behalf of your faith tradition, especially since there are many fears and misapprehensions over the procedure. From the point of view of the transplant team and the specialist nurse, discussions are carried out in a sensitive manner so that families can be fully informed to make a decision. At times, people simply agree without really thinking about what donation means and then feel that they have not been fully informed as the process is carried out. This may be the case in, for instance, donation by circulatory criteria for death when it may be sometime before treatment is withdrawn and the patient may not die in a timeframe that allows for donation. Sometimes it may seem to families that however careful the medical team is, a decision has already been made or that pressure is being put on them. The chaplain who is secure in his faith tradition can help here to communicate and reflect the different voices in the discussion. The chaplain can also reassure relatives that they can say their goodbyes and fulfil any necessary religious rituals or traditions for their dying loved one.

When a person is drifting in and out of consciousness they may not be aware of what is going on around them. However, research shows that people may still hear. Arguments or unnecessary chatting may be disrespectful at a time when someone is dying. Although Kim and Mike could benefit from the chaplain's calming presence, the chaplain may wish to consider his priorities – Joan appears to be imminently dying, and a significant aspect of her spiritual care is anointing. She has shown her consent by squeezing the chaplain's hand. Any ritual or sacrament should be done in prayerful context and preferably with the attendance of the family and close friends. Where this is not possible, the chaplain should anoint. The chaplain's duty is to Joan and her spiritual care is his primary concern.

Prayer in these circumstances is not simply about guidance on how to make the right decision. The chaplain is here to minister to Liam who may or may not be dying but who still has spiritual needs, and Liam's parents who are facing an uncertain future for their son and a sense of loss that may eventually lead to bereavement. Observing that the situation is evolving and not necessarily fixed may help you to clarify the different stages and how things may unfold for Liam. Engaging with Liam by talking to him, even if he is unconscious, and praying with him can give encouragement to his parents who may be finding it difficult to let go of the person they think he once was and embrace the person he is. In these circumstances, giving time to talk through what is happening, to try and make sense and not to rush into decisions will help Mr and Mrs Kelly better to come to terms with what the future holds for Liam. Remember, this is only the beginning of your journey with Mr and Mrs Kelly and with Liam so accompany them as they approach each new stage. As this may be a long journey, consider what you can offer and do not be afraid to call in the chaplaincy team for help.

REFLECTION

What is a good death for you? Why?

Summary

Most people do not want to think about their dying and death. Although the decision to carry an organ donation card has been widely promoted, people often do not think about discussing what they do and do not want with their families and loved ones. Frequently something like a television programme will prompt an offhand comment such as, 'If ever I get like that, shoot me'. But this is not a useful indication of what the person really thinks. In many cases we do not know what we would want until we are actually in that situation and find that we can adjust well to our new reality. Nor can we think easily about our own death. We have only our experience of the death of other people to inform us on this. Many people in hospital find that their illness forces them to think about death and it puts their life into perspective. Even if this is not the start of the conversation with the chaplain, frequently this is where the discussion goes. In the Resources section there is a useful online resource called the Art of Dying Well. This resource reminds us that dying well begins in living well. Thinking about death and taking time to plan can still be a part of cherishing life and good stewardship.

In the next chapter, we turn to some of the ethical decisions that we may be faced with as we near the end of life.

Chapter 9

DYING AND DEATH
ETHICAL ISSUES

CASE STUDY

The chaplain has been supporting Malcolm and Nora Osborne for several months, ever since Nora first came to the hospital for a series of blood tests, memory tests and scans. While Nora is having a further scan, Malcolm chats to the chaplain who is rapidly becoming a good friend. Malcolm explains that Nora has finally been diagnosed with dementia, although Malcolm says he has expected this for some time. Malcolm finds that caring for his wife on his own is becoming more and more difficult, especially when she often does not seem to recognise him. He does not want to involve their grown children in her care, because he does not want Nora to be a burden on the family. Malcolm has decided that he cannot bear to see his wife go through any more suffering, and he does not want to carry on without her so he tells the chaplain that he is thinking of taking her to a clinic in Switzerland where they both can end their lives 'with dignity'. Malcolm thinks this is the most compassionate thing to do in the circumstances. Before he rejoins his wife, Malcolm asks if the chaplain, as his friend, would help him find out about possible clinics and if the chaplain would give him and Nora his blessing.

As the chaplain leaves Malcolm, Olga, a nurse, asks for a chat and a bit of advice. One of Olga's patients, Pat, is in a terminal phase of her illness. Olga explains that Pat's relatives vehemently believe in the sanctity of life, and they want everything done for Pat, including putting in a percutaneous endoscopic gastrostomy tube to enable her to be fed. Olga and the doctors think that this will not benefit Pat, and Olga is trying to work out how to communicate this to the relatives in the most sensitive way.

> ### REFLECTION
> Is living well about having as much time as possible? Is living well deliberately cutting life short by hastening death?

End-of-life care and dying

When thinking about ethical issues involved in end-of-life care, we have to keep in mind both respect for life and acceptance of death. Respect for life reminds us of the dignity that all people have throughout their lives. One implication of this is that we should never intentionally aim to bring about a person's death. Acceptance of death reminds us that we should all prepare properly for death. One implication of this is that we should accept the reality of the situation, and this has an effect on the kind of treatment we should pursue.

Respect for the person who is nearing death involves respecting the person's beliefs, wishes and values as well as respecting the person's life. Historically, this holistic approach has been implicit in care of the dying since this care has always been part of religious care. This is well illustrated by the hospice movement, which developed from the medieval practice of religious houses that cared for the sick and travellers into the modern hospices that were set up by deeply religious people such as Dame Cicely Saunders. Pastoral care of people who are dying and their relatives is a staple part of the work of the healthcare chaplain. The process of dying is complex because it involves the whole person, including their relationships, and yet at the same time it seems that it is more than the whole person. Accompanying and supporting someone who is dying is being given permission to encounter the person in what may be the most sacred space of hopes, dreams, fears and secrets. Care of the dying is a great privilege.

Ensuring that patients are actively involved in discussions about their care and that decisions on behalf of competent patients are not made without their consent are important ethical aspects of respect for the person. However, although it can never become routine, chaplains are used to talking about dying, but they may find that patients are not. Nor can the chaplain make assumptions about whether or not the patient has a religious faith. Generally speaking, and for many reasons, people are rather reluctant to talk about dying and death. Since most people do not die in their own homes, dying and death tend to be hidden out of view; since many people are living well into their 80s it is easy to keep dying out of mind. Of course, no one knows precisely when they are going to die. However, a visit to a hospital may change our perspective, and we may suddenly realise how ill-prepared we are for what is, after all, an inevitable part of living. Nevertheless, people may not know how to start a conversation about spirituality or they may think that spirituality and the work of the chaplain are purely for patients who are obviously religious. Spiritual care attends to the patient as a person, to the patient's formal religious care if that is required, but also to their existential care and their personal questioning and search for meaning. Once we see spirituality as part and parcel of a person's very being then this can open up into a personal encounter.

Accepting that we are going to die may cause us to think about how we are living now, about relationships, about our priorities, about spirituality and about the possibility of a life to come. It may also help us to think about how we would like to say goodbye to those we love. For those who have been diagnosed with a serious illness and for their families there is uncertainty and anxiety as well as challenges, but there is also often the realisation that life is both a precious and a precarious gift and that the simplest things often become the things that give joy.

Dying well begins with living well, with valuing life, with attending to the spiritual as well as bodily aspects of our life. Having the conversation about dying well is an important part of end-of-life care, and this includes patients, their family and those who are closest to them. There are new initiatives to encourage people to think about how to prepare for the end of life, to reflect on what it means to them to die well, and you can find some of these in the Resources section. Thinking about your death or coming to terms with a final illness is an intensely personal experience with no right or wrong way to go about it. There may be an acute sense of loss and grief about what will never be, but there also may be the possibility of enjoying life right up until the last moment.

When people think that they may be facing a life-limiting illness more often than not they value an honest and open conversation about dying and death. Truth telling is a moral obligation and information should be communicated with respect and sensitivity, while holding at the same time that it is important to choose the right time to talk and to give the right amount of detail for that particular patient. This balance may be difficult to strike and no healthcare professional wants to give false hope or take away all hope. However, often patients give cues as to what they are thinking and feeling and how much they wants to know. Good, sensitive and clear communication, and involving the family in conversations with the permission of the patient, is an important part of the process.

End-of-life care is not simply about caring for people in the last moments of their life. It also includes supporting people who are in the last months or even years of their life. This means that end-of-life care can take place in a person's own home, in a care home, a hospice or a hospital or a combination of these places, and it is not always certain that the chaplain will be on hand. Nevertheless, spiritual care is central to care in any of these different settings. It is also useful for the chaplain to be familiar with palliative care, because even though palliative care can begin at any time in a person's illness, this kind of care is an important part of good end-of-life care. Palliative care makes a person as comfortable as possible by managing pain and distress and this kind of care recognises that explaining what is happening and what may happen can help people deal with their fears. But palliative care also includes psychological, social, emotional and spiritual support for the person and for the person's family and carers, and it extends into bereavement support. Being aware of the way in which spiritual distress manifests itself, whether it be physical, emotional or existential, or simply restlessness, is essential in order to support the patient effectively.

Information: dying and definitions

Healthcare ethics requires that we make accurate distinctions. At times we get a little confused about dying. Although it is true to say that 'we are all dying', in another sense this is not the case. Someone, for instance, with a diagnosis of dementia is not dying, nor is dementia a death sentence. In fact, there is good research and resources to show how people with dementia can live well and fully. Moreover, it is notoriously difficult to predict how long terminally ill people have to live. We are also a little confused over some of the terms to describe dying and death, and the word *euthanasia* is a good example. In the original Greek, euthanasia meant *eu* (good or easy) and *thanatos* (death). However, now 'euthanasia' means, in a popular sense, to end a person's life in order to put an end to that person's suffering, and we can no longer return to the original meaning of euthanasia without great confusion. Euthanasia in this popular sense is unlawful in the UK.

Nevertheless, some interpretations of the popular meaning also cause confusion – some people make a distinction between 'active euthanasia' where a person deliberately and directly causes the death of the patient (for instance, by injecting poison) and 'passive euthanasia' when, for instance, life-sustaining treatment is withdrawn from a patient. The use of this language of active and passive to describe euthanasia is quite persuasive but misinformed. These terms are usually used both by those who insist on prolonging life no matter what (vitalists), so that withdrawal of, for example, life support is an act that kills, and by those who wish to advocate euthanasia (in its popular meaning), who also maintain that society already accepts euthanasia and yet is being 'dishonest' in not admitting it. Euthanasia can indeed be brought about by an action or by an omission when there is an intention to bring about the death of the patient in order to eliminate all suffering. However, when treatment is withdrawn because it is no longer appropriate for this patient, for example it is futile, the intention is not to bring about the patient's death. In this situation, the intention is to stop futile treatment in the knowledge that the patient may die – this is not euthanasia. Some people think that intentions are far too obscure to help in these situations. But imagine that you have withdrawn treatment and the patient does not die – if you are irritated that the patient is still alive and begin to think of other occasions when you can withdraw treatment, that says something about your intention; if, however, you rejoice that the patient is still alive then we can assume you did not intend to bring about their death.

Vitalists and those who are pro-euthanasia tend not to accept that there is a clear and valid distinction between killing and letting die. However, it is inaccurate to use the term 'euthanasia' (in its popular sense) for letting the (dying) patient die a timely death from an underlying pathological condition. Rather, this is to acknowledge that our lives on earth are limited and everything comes to a natural end. When a patient is allowed to die from an underlying condition, when nothing more can be done for them or when treatment is considered too burdensome or extraordinary and so optional, then this is not 'death by omission' – rather, we cease doing what was once called for and we continue to care but in a way that is called for now. We care for the dying.

There are some other common definitions: we can distinguish between *involuntary euthanasia* – when the person who dies wants to live but is killed anyway; *non-voluntary euthanasia* – where the person is unable to ask for euthanasia (they may be unconscious) or to make a meaningful choice between living and dying and another person takes the decision on their behalf (this may be according to a living will or previously expressed wishes); *voluntary euthanasia* – euthanasia is carried out at the request of the person who dies.

Technically *physician-assisted suicide* is not euthanasia, because the patient needs help to kill themselves, but it is the patient who commits the final act by, for example, administering drugs provided by the doctor. In euthanasia another person does the final act. *Assisted suicide* suggests that a person who is not a medical professional helps someone, though the final act remains the act of that someone. For those who promote a change in the law to allow for assisted suicide the preferred term is *assisted dying*. This term is used by those who think that there is a stigma attached to suicide and so object to suicide being associated with assistance to die. However, assisted dying leaves open the possibility that the final act can be done by someone other than the person seeking assistance in dying, and so it would in fact be an act of euthanasia.

Euthanasia as deliberate and direct killing is unlawful in the UK, and the law treats it as murder: *mercy killing* is not a defence. In English law, assisted suicide is illegal. The Netherlands and Belgium are two of the few countries in the world where euthanasia is openly practised. In Switzerland, euthanasia is illegal, but someone who assists in another person's suicide will not necessarily be prosecuted if that person did not act from selfish motives.

Until 1961, *suicide* or self-murder was a crime in the UK. A person who failed in an attempt to commit suicide could be prosecuted and even sent to prison. Attitudes to people who were suicidal began to change in the 1950s and with the medicalisation of suicide came the view that rather than imprisonment, those who attempted suicide required proper treatment for mental distress. As a result of this change in attitude, under section 1 of the Suicide Act 1961 suicide ceased to be a crime. However, under section 2 of the Act, doing an act with the intention that it will encourage or assist another person's suicide remains a criminal offence and whether or not the person is prosecuted is a matter for the Crown Prosecution Service.

The high rates of suicide have led many governments to see suicide as a real problem for public health. This is because it affects not only the person committing suicide but also the family, people who witness suicide or find the person too late, paramedics and police who have to deal with the situation and subsequent generations who may be haunted by suicide as also a possibility for them. Governments have come to see that suicide prevention is a matter for everyone and in 2012 the Department of Health put in place a Suicide Prevention Strategy to support the bereaved and to prevent suicide among at-risk groups. Among other things, the Suicide Prevention Strategy recognises the need to reduce opportunities for suicide, for instance by redesigning buildings and ensuring that potentially lethal drugs are prescribed safely. The Strategy also wants to see better support for people at high risk of suicidal attempts such as people with mental health problems and people who self-harm. Building up life skills, such as coping skills, developing resilience and self-esteem, stress management, problem-solving and critical thinking are key to a comprehensive approach to suicide prevention.

Suicide or controlling death?

Some patients who are faced with the possibility of a difficult death or with what they see as living in an undignified situation would rather have control over the timing of their death. A patient may ask a doctor to assist them to end their life. As we have seen, assisting in a person's suicide remains unlawful even if the person requests it. However, some people argue that a request for help in dying such as being given a prescription for lethal medication is not assistance in suicide. Rather it is a choice by a dying person about how and when their life should end. In order to think this through we may want to consider precisely to what extent patient choice does rule the way in which medicine is governed. After all, a patient can refuse treatment, but the patient cannot demand it. We may want to reflect on the doctor's role as healer and the commitment to do no harm. This may lead us to question whether helping to bring about the patient's death is really compatible with the vocation of medicine. We may want to think about what lies behind a person's choice for death – palliative care can address symptoms of pain and suffering. However, the concern of many people is no longer pain management. Rather, it is existential suffering, the sense of being a burden, losing control, lacking meaning in life.

Often the positive support that the chaplain offers is forgotten in these difficult situations. Some people incorrectly think that chaplains are only available for people with strong and established faith beliefs. Some mistakenly assume that the chaplain will try to convert or preach at a patient who is in a particularly vulnerable state. In reality, chaplains have the expertise to engage with patients in a way that can get to the root of why the patient fears a lack of autonomy or control over what is happening, why they feel isolated, without support and without dignity, why they can no longer find meaning. Facing terminal illness, dying and death need not necessarily mean giving up all control. Helping the patient and their families talk about how the patient wants to spend their final days can open up new possibilities. In the art of dying well, good palliative care has a central place. So too do relationships, understanding loved ones in a different way, opening up communication and discovering graced moments.

Making decisions

In Chapter 3 we saw that if a competent patient refuses treatment, then their refusal is respected, even if it means that the patient will die. We also saw that if a patient has made a legal and valid advance decision, that decision will be followed when the patient no longer has capacity. In Chapter 4 we discussed decision-making for the patient who no longer has capacity and who has not made an advance decision. We noted that, under the Mental Capacity Act, doctors have a duty to act in the best interests of the patient in consultation with the patient's family and close friends. In discussions with the family, the chaplain is often well placed to give time and to manage the emotional stress that such decision-making involves, especially where there is no agreement. Relatives unprepared for the death of their loved one may ask doctors to do absolutely everything medically possible. But what the relatives often mean is to give their loved one back the life they used to have. Sometimes doing everything possible is a way in which relatives manage their guilt about not doing enough in the past or they think it is a way of demonstrating their love and commitment. One of the most difficult decisions to make is deciding whether to withdraw or withhold treatment that could prolong life.

Withdrawing or withholding treatment

With advancements in technology, life-prolonging medicine seems to be becoming more extreme and people are often worried about spending their last months or days connected to machines keeping them alive. People fear the dying process. This fear may lead some people to refuse even treatment that is of benefit to them. One response to this is to recognise that medicine has its limits and to agree that patients do not have to undergo aggressive or futile treatments. While a doctor should not deliberately aim to bring about the death of the patient, the doctor does not have a duty to treat a patient when treatment is futile or burdensome. However, it may be useful to think in terms of fostering an attitude that opts for life first. We should also be aware that it is notoriously difficult to predict when people are going to die. In addition to an accurate diagnosis and opportunities for regular reassesments where necessary, good and sensitive communication is essential for a decision to withdraw or withhold treatment to be implemented well. Generally, this decision should be made by the patient or someone with the legal power to act for the patient. Involving the family where this is appropriate and with the consent of the patient may alleviate the fear that the medical profession is simply giving up, and so it may significantly help the family come to terms with what is happening.

Nutrition and hydration

Cooking for people, eating with them and feeding people are hugely significant human acts – it is what we do for those for whom we care. This is perhaps why issues to do with nutrition and hydration in particular seem to be ethically fraught. Even when a patient loses interest in food and fluids, continuing to feed in principle should not be neglected, and it should be done with attentiveness to their needs. Risks such as that of choking need to be assessed; however, excessive attention either to risk or the labour-intensive time it takes to help someone eat should not be factors in whether or not to withdraw oral feeding.

In English law, clinically assisted nutrition and hydration (CANH) is different from helping people eat and drink orally in that CANH includes intravenous feeding, feeding by nasogastric tube, by percutaneous endoscopic gastrostomy or radiologically inserted gastrostomy feeding tubes through the abdominal wall. In English law, CANH is regarded as medical treatment. However, many people see nutrition and hydration as the normal care we give people whether it is delivered orally or by clinical assistance. This means that any clinical decision regarding the provision of CANH should be discussed with especial sensitivity to the concerns of the patient or relatives and reasons should be clearly communicated. The death of the patient must never be the aim of withdrawing or withholding food or fluids.

Case study: ethical implications

See: Many people wish to take control of a situation because they make assumptions about the realities or because they do not want to ask for help. Some people may not even think that what they are planning is unethical, and in cases involving end-of-life issues often people convince themselves that there are no alternatives. Seeing the situation as it is will enable new avenues to be found. However, when a chaplain is in a relationship of friendship, does it become more difficult to disagree with the friend's proposed course of action? Is taking someone who does not have capacity to consent for assisted suicide really a true description of the act? If the chaplain helps someone in their suicide, even if this is providing information, is this cooperation in an evil act on the part of the chaplain?

Judge: Did safeguarding come into your mind?

Act: Consider how you can give people the language for talking about the sanctity of life in a way that honours life but also acknowledges that our life lies in the future with God. How do you offer hope to people in what appears to be a hopeless situation? Have you offered to accompany Pat and her family on their difficult journey?

Some further comments

In the case study, you should *see* that safeguarding is once again a significant issue, and an important question for the chaplain is whether Nora is indeed in danger. After all, even though Nora does not seem to be aware of Malcolm's plans and possibly does not have capacity to agree to them, assisted suicide and euthanasia are unlawful, and this assistance includes travelling to a country where these acts are permitted. Once again, the chaplain needs to consider the safeguarding policy of the institution and *judge* whether anything needs to be put in place to protect Nora. Certainly, if Malcolm wants to go ahead and find out more information about euthanasia clinics, the chaplain cannot facilitate this process. However, it does not appear that Malcolm has made a definite plan, and so the chaplain may want to explore the situation further with Malcolm. The sacred space between the chaplain and the person is not only sacred, it is also safe. This means safe in terms of safeguarding vulnerable people. But it also means that in that space people can explore and express feelings without fear of judgement. The person can say what is in their heart. When things reach crisis point a person may express pent up feelings that lie hidden behind their statements. By responding to what is being said in an open way, the chaplain can reflect back so that the person can hear what they are saying and identify more clearly what they are feeling. This *act* of active listening is not problem-solving, or taking on responsibility for the person's life, or being in charge or making decisions for other people or fixing situations. In tuning in to the person, the chaplain provides a caring presence and offers up a mirror to that person.

When someone talks about wanting death with dignity this is an opportunity to open up the discussion not shut it down. It enables a conversation about what are the person's needs, what help is available, about practicalities. In particular, listen out for reasons to live among the reasons that the person gives to die. Malcolm talks about not wanting his family to see Nora as a burden. This in itself demonstrates that family are important to Malcolm and Nora so a conversation is to be had about what family life means to them. Moreover, a diagnosis of dementia is not a death sentence. Finding support groups and becoming better informed about options may help Malcolm and Nora to make a life plan instead of a plan for death.

When people speak about wanting to avoid burdening others with their care, what lies underneath this is often more to do with a sense of pride and control – some people do not want to rely on others. Some people simply do not want others to see their vulnerability or need. Some people may be caught up in what they perceive to be the stigma of certain illnesses such as dementia.

However, worries about how the family will cope, about being a burden, are real concerns that need to be voiced. Talking things through with someone who is not a family member may be easier because that someone is at distance from the situation.

In advising Olga, the chaplain can remind her that any decisions regarding treatment are to be made by the patient as far as is possible, and the patient is to be supported in making the decision. If Pat is an adult and has capacity, then she can refuse treatment, and this includes hydration and nutrition. In cases where a competent patient who is not dying refuses clinically assisted nutrition and hydration and cannot be persuaded by the healthcare team that CANH would be beneficial for them, then the healthcare team is not guilty of neglect in not providing CANH – the law takes the decision out of their hands. However, this does not appear to be Pat's situation, since it is the relatives who want everything to be done for Pat. Assuming then that Pat does not have capacity to make a decision about her treatment, and Pat has not made an advance directive or appointed a lasting power of attorney, the healthcare team must act in her best interests. To help them identify her best interests, the team should consult with relatives and those closest to Pat. The chaplain's expertise may be useful here, especially when it comes to talking around the subject of the sanctity of life. Many people take sanctity of life in a vitalist way and so wish to hold on to life no matter what. The chaplain is well placed to enable the relatives to reflect on what the sanctity of life means to them, to explore the limits of life as well as how to cherish and honour life. In particular, the chaplain can open up a conversation about the experience of dying and death and what dying well for Pat and for her relatives may mean.

Olga says that Pat is in the terminal phase of her illness. The chaplain may want to explore with Olga whether or not she thinks that Pat is in the last days of her life. It is very difficult to say precisely when someone is near death but stopping food and fluids with the intention of shortening a patient's life is unethical. The provision of nutrition and hydration ordinarily sustains the patient's life and, moreover, it has special significance for many families. Withdrawing or withholding nutrition and hydration seems to be an abandonment of the patient and a sign of giving up. One thing Olga may wish to consider is whether Pat can still be given adequate food and drink orally. If this is no longer the case, and Pat is indeed dying, then since in principle CANH should be provided to meet Pat's nutritional needs the team must be very clear why CANH has ceased to be clinically indicated. This must be judged on the basis of Pat's needs, and nutrition and hydration should be assessed separately. Above all, a decision to withhold CANH cannot be motivated by the intention to shorten Pat's life. Given the concerns of the relatives it may be prudential for the team to discuss with the relatives the different kinds of CANH and their accompanying risks and benefits. Pat's relatives may be unwilling to face the idea that Pat is dying but they may also be truly concerned that withholding nutrition and hydration will in fact bring about her death. They may also be worried about a misdiagnosis of imminent death. Sensitivity towards these concerns and a willingness to discuss different avenues as well as an openness to reassess the situation may help in the communication process. A conversation about good palliative care, care that honours and opts for life, may help Pat and her family as they face Pat's final journey.

Inviting people to **p**ray with you as well as the prayer you pray yourself can be a powerful way of reminding people that God recognises their struggles but he does not leave them alone. A careful prayer can help a person to name their difficulties and to acknowledge their dependence on God and on others. Prayer and deep relationship with God allows for accepting the people we are and the people we meet. **O**bserve the positive in situations, especially when other people only see the darkness. **E**ngaging with people where they are opens up the possibility for a deeper discussion that can name and describe fears so that they can be faced. Sometimes you have to be aware of **t**ime and timing, especially when it is a matter of safeguarding. **R**emember to check back on people and to arrange follow-up meetings.

You should be aware of the burdens that end-of-life care places on others but also on yourself. We often remind people that no one is a burden but then think that we are a burden on others if we feel we need to depend on them. Talk to your colleagues.

> REFLECTION
>
> What treatment would you want as you approach death? Does autonomy have the last say?

Summary

Some of the more prominent ethical questions arise as people near the end of life, notably questions of hastening death, cooperation in acts that are unethical and the ethics of foregoing life-sustaining treatment. However, there are also the ethics surrounding honest communication, keeping care personal, building up trust, asking about spirituality and exploring priorities and choice. Ensuring that the person's privacy and dignity are promoted and addressing distressing symptoms are important aspects of good person-centred care. Moreover, good ongoing care for the family can make a significant difference as their loved one nears death and after the person has died. In the next chapter, we look at ethical issues in grief and bereavement.

Chapter 10

LOSS, GRIEF AND BEREAVEMENT, BURN-OUT AND THE WOUNDED HEALER

CASE STUDY

A member of the chaplaincy team is in the process of preparing the hospital chapel for a service. She finds a nurse, Queenie, sitting at the back. Queenie has clearly been crying. Queenie explains that she and her husband have been diagnosed with unexplained infertility. They have tried IVF, and it has not worked. She recently had her last IVF embryo implanted, but she miscarried, and so she has been off work. They now know that they will never have their own children. Queenie blames herself, because she thinks that God has punished her for trying to 'play God' by going through IVF. As the chaplain leaves the chapel, one of Queenie's colleagues, Rachael, comes up. Rachael knows that Queenie has had time off work and is upset. She also says that she thinks Queenie has been drinking more alcohol than usual. Rachael wants to help her friend out and asks the chaplain what is going on and what she can do.

On the ward, Simon is finding it very difficult to deal with Tim. Tim is 42 and has severe learning difficulties. He lives in a specially adapted community home supported by his carer Udi. Tim does not speak, though he can verbalise. Tim has come in for a routine operation, but he is not settling. He paces up and down the room. He tries the door handles. He seems to want to leave. Udi says he has never seen Tim so anxious and restless and uncooperative, and he does not know what is wrong. Simon wonders if the chaplain could help. The chaplain has just come from the bedside of a patient who is dying, and he arrives still wearing his dog collar and carrying his stole. On seeing him, Tim cowers in the corner of the room. The chaplain takes Udi aside for a chat, and he asks if anything particular has changed in Tim's routine. Udi replies that Tim has been a bit withdrawn for a few months. Tim had been very close to his mother who used to visit him frequently. It turns out that Tim's mother had died, but his family had decided it would be best not to tell Tim, since he probably would not understand and might be upset. In order to provide an explanation for why Tim's mother was not visiting him, the family asked the care staff to tell Tim that his mother was in hospital.

> ### REFLECTION
>
> How often does my interpretation of what is happening and how I would want to respond to a situation colour how I deal with other people?

Loss, grief and bereavement

It hardly needs to be said that throughout life we face losses of one kind or another. Some losses are significant, others less so. Some losses affect one person more deeply than another. In the Jewish tradition, coping with losses throughout life is a bit like boiling an egg – a boiled egg symbolises hope because, like the boiled egg, we can become more resilient. However, for most people the shock of the death of a loved one is one of the deepest losses and one that can cause the most spiritual distress. Death may be expected, waited for, and in some cases hoped for, yet it always comes as a shock. It is the shock of finality.

In Chapter 9, we reflected on the idea that dying well begins with living well, with valuing life, with attending to the spiritual as well as bodily aspects of our life. Once we have a perspective on cherishing life while also recognising that our life on earth is limited, we can have a better perspective on dying well. In a similar way, care for people who experience loss, grief and bereavement begins by engaging with them throughout their loved one's last journey and not simply after the patient has died. Care for the dying patient encompasses care for their family, significant friends and carers. This care entails consideration of how someone is coping with caring and the demands of the situation as well as the impending bereavement. Grief often begins before the loved one has died. Accompanying people throughout this period and recognising their grief can help them so that they can make wise decisions regarding treatment. Wise decision-making can help people to feel that they did what was truly and properly required of them in the circumstances. Of course, sometimes the chaplain has not been in a position to accompany family and friends through the dying process. Nevertheless, there is a way of accompanying through talking about and remembering what has happened. Above all, the chaplain is asked to respect people's individuality in grieving.

Certainly, spiritual support need not be formally structured, and assessing a person's spiritual needs often comes about over numerous conversations. However, many organisations are developing their own formal assessment tools that are designed to be quick and easy to use. Although nurses tend to be among the first healthcare practitioners to identify patients who may present with a spiritual need, chaplains are regarded as the main spiritual care providers and one aspect of the chaplain's work is to carry out spiritual care assessments. Assessments are not only for patients, they are also for those close to them. There is merit in assessing the spiritual needs of people who are facing bereavement since an assessment that is properly carried out and that activates appropriate support can help to head off later problems. Nevertheless, there are inherent dangers in any formal tool in that they can become simply tick-box exercises or activities that are done only once and so do not take account of changing needs.

In caring for someone who is dying, family and carers often move between the day-to-day practicalities of caring and then being overwhelmed by feelings of sadness, guilt, anger, powerlessness and hopelessness. This natural movement of head and heart can be an indication of resilience, while powerful and persistent feelings of being overwhelmed may signal vulnerability. Some people have the inner resources to cope and this, combined with the support of family and friends, can help with the bereavement process. Since bereavement is a natural process, people who are resilient may not need extra support. In contrast, other people may be more vulnerable and they may be more affected by the experience of death or they may suffer feelings of guilt or blame. Grief takes on many different guises and it can be a part of the normal process of losing a loved one or it can become overly complicated. A person may grieve for a few days, weeks, months or even years. To a certain extent, it is not the length of time that matters, rather it is the severity of grief and how grief impacts on a person's life. People who are really struggling with grief or where grief has an impact on their daily living may require professional support.

Information: grief and bereavement

The way in which a person is told that their loved one has died can have tremendous impact and it often stays in the person's memory. Unless there are obvious reasons to the contrary, having a chaplain present is useful, even if the family or deceased have shown no interest in religion or spirituality, since the chaplain can always give the family time and space. Where possible, this sort of news should be delivered face to face, although frequently the news is broken on the telephone. Sensitivity to the person on the other end of the line is crucial, especially if they are already vulnerable, for instance if they are elderly or on their own. In some cases, healthcare professionals have tried to mitigate bad news by saying that the patient woke up happy and then just slipped away. This may backfire if the relative knows perfectly well that their loved one never woke up happy, and any slight deviation from the truth may cause the relative to doubt further information. Ideally, the news is given in a private and confidential space, free from possible interruption and with plenty of time available. Simple and clear language is best to convey the message, and the person should be encouraged to express their feelings if that is what they want.

Since spiritual care assessments are formally recorded and made in partnership with the individuals concerned, an assessment should follow the protocol of the chaplain's organisation and explicit consent from the patient or individual is required. The chaplain making the assessment should make it clear that the person can opt out at any stage. Confidentiality remains central, as do the requirements of data protection.

When a person shares their story of loss and grief, the response of the chaplain can only be a respectful listening. There can be no 'fixing' by the professional, because these are stories of brokenness and sorrow, of how loss has changed and unravelled the pattern of daily life. In a narrative where caring works alongside storytelling there is a cognitive approach that attempts to help the person adjust to new realities by reflecting on the story and rethinking the narrative. There is also dialogue and support for the person who struggles with the idea of change. But such narratives go further in allowing the grief-stricken person to witness the profundity and mystery of the experience of loss. The person is listened to and heard.

There are procedures to be followed after the death of a patient, and the chaplain should be familiar with any protocols specific to his organisation or workplace. When family members are already in shock over the death of their loved one, extra procedures may seem to be irrelevant or obstructive. These feelings may add to the distress of the person who is bereaved. A gentle explanation of some of the processes may help to reduce feelings of bewilderment. Although the patient has died, respect and reverence for the deceased remains. Respect for the dead body is a sign of respect for life and for the person who is now gone. How we deal then with a dead body is an ethical issue, and at all times the body must be treated with utmost respect and care so that dignity and privacy are maintained.

Unexpected death

If death has been unexpected and sudden, the deceased patient and immediate surroundings should be left undisturbed until a duty doctor has confirmed and recorded the death. If the doctor is concerned about any of the circumstances, then the police, as representatives of the coroner, may be called. Support must be given to the family at this time, in particular by explaining the process and next steps. The family may wish to see their loved one, but they will require police permission if any of the circumstances raise concerns.

If the cause of death is known, is a natural cause and the patient was seen by a doctor within 14 days prior to death (a patient rushed suddenly into hospital may not have been seen by a doctor), then a death certificate can be issued without referral to the coroner. Otherwise, the death is reported to the coroner who makes enquiries into the identity of the deceased, the time and place of death, and how death occurred. The coroner may issue a death certificate or the coroner may order a post mortem. If the post mortem establishes that death was by natural causes, then a death certificate may be issued. If there is doubt, then an inquest may be held. If a post mortem is required, then any tubes, lines and catheters are left in place.

Expected death

Usually, when death is expected, a note is made in the patient records and the family are made aware of the situation. Once again, it is good practice to document communication with the next of kin. Again, as part of good practice, the spiritual, religious, cultural and practical wishes of the dying patient should be recorded.

Personal care of the patient after death ('last offices')

Once the death of the patient has been confirmed and the family or next of kin informed, the family will be asked if they would like to see their loved one and if they wish to see the chaplain. Relatives may also be asked if they would like to assist in the final personal care of the deceased, including being washed and dressed appropriately.

At this time, rituals may be very useful ways of holding the tension for what has happened. Reciting prayers, taking time to prepare the body with care and sensitivity, following specific practices such as washing or wrapping the body, are ways in which all those taking part show respect and care for the person who has died.

Mourning

While bereavement is associated with the experience of loss, and grief is the emotional stress that accompanies bereavement, mourning is usually seen as a social expression of grief or bereavement. Mourning often takes on specific cultural or religious forms and in order to minister effectively the chaplain should be aware of these different forms. Moreover, different cultures show different expectations of displays of emotion and grief, and this difference may also extend to the gender of the person. Individual situations may also affect grief and mourning. Take, for instance, the death of an elderly person who has been expected to die. This elderly person has accepted dying, has said all their goodbyes and put everything including their relationships in order. Although their death remains a shock for the family, there is some comfort in knowing that this was a death in season. Contrast this with the unexpected death of a baby. Research has shown that grief and bereavement lasts longer for parents who have lost babies and children. Often parents experience social isolation, loss of control, meaning and purpose, sometimes even loss of feelings of worth. The two examples in the case study illustrate that grief and mourning do not have rules that must be followed and that people grieve in their own different ways.

The chaplain may also wish to consider healthcare colleagues. Often nurses in particular know the patient well, even though the patient and their family are outside the nurse's social structure and life. The death of the patient, especially after long and intimate nursing, may cause feelings of grief and profound sadness, but the nurse may not have a way of expressing this formally, and there may be no connection with the mourning process. It may also be difficult for the professional to share this with other people or with the family. By working as a team, chaplains and their colleagues can support each other.

Response to grief

Reactions to grief range widely and they can include physical symptoms of palpitations, sleep disturbance, crying and nausea; emotional responses of anger, denial, guilt, blame, hopelessness, loneliness and fear; cognitive effects of indifference to normal activities, confusion, poor concentration and numbness; behavioural reactions of changes in sleep or appetite, searching or social withdrawal. Often there have been hidden difficulties in the family, especially where there have been difficulties with the person who has died. These issues now surface, and if not dealt with sensitively, they may cause further damage. Taking time with the family with supportive listening, encouragement, practical support where necessary is all important when it comes to mending the heart.

Boundaries

A person who is grieving may be vulnerable. This means that the chaplain, as always, must behave professionally and maintain appropriate boundaries. Things to consider include being careful not to give out your home telephone number or personal mobile number. Check that the timing of meetings is convenient and make a record of meetings or calls. Be aware of the difficulties in supporting several members of a family. Families have their own momentum and the family history often means that each person has a particular place. The danger for the chaplain is either to become lost in the sympathy and grief or to remain detached and therefore unapproachable. Moreover, when the chaplain witnesses the rawness of fear, sadness, loneliness and loss this may remind him of his own experiences of loss or unresolved issues.

Part of understanding boundaries and engaging in reflective practice involves knowing our own grieving process and the way it may limit our life, and then using this as a resource and not as an interference in supporting others. Of course, the chaplain's involvement with the grieving family will come to a natural end, and it is important to recognise that this may feel like another loss.

Case study: ethical implications

See: In working out a good description of what is happening the chaplain may have to put aside some of his own assumptions and create an ethical space in which to appreciate the particular significance the circumstances have for the people involved. The significance of miscarriage is a good example of this, since miscarriage is often seen as either an invisible or even an insignificant loss. Attentive listening is an ethical requirement here so that the situation can be adequately assessed.

Judge: The chaplain should always be mindful of the ethical importance of confidentiality. In most cases, people do act out of good intentions. Although a skilled chaplain may judge that certain problems could have been averted, judging the people involved will not help move the situation on.

Act: Everyone has spiritual needs. As part of your professional development consider how you can minister more effectively to people who present with apparently challenging behaviour. You may just find that the perceived challenge exists only because other people lack the appropriate skills and communication strategies, and it is often easier to designate the person a challenge rather than look to our own inadequacies. Is this not an ethical issue of promoting the dignity of the person? Sometimes the action in grief and bereavement is simply looking with the bereaved person at possible ways of 'being' in this situation.

Some further comments

Miscarriage, the loss of pregnancy before 20 weeks, is often an invisible and lonely loss, because in many cases only a very few people are aware that the woman was expecting a baby, and the loss itself may be invisible – there is often nothing tangible to grieve. Queenie's situation involves not only the loss of this baby but also a sense of loss for her future, since she knows that she will never become a mother. Many women who have had a miscarriage describe their central feeling as emptiness. Helping Queenie put her feelings of guilt to rest is important, especially where she feels that she has been punished. Although the chaplain should *see* and be aware of where his faith tradition stands on the procedure of IVF, his concern is with the grief and loss that Queenie is undergoing. Queenie's feelings of grief may come and go, and they may last for some time, so the chaplain may want to suggest further meetings. Rachael's concern for Queenie may be understandable, but the chaplain has to *judge* and above all remember the requirements of confidentiality. Under these requirements, the chaplain is not at liberty to comment on Queenie's situation. The chaplain cannot say that he has even met with Queenie, nor can he disclose what Queenie has said or comment on what has happened to her. Nor can the chaplain assume that Queenie would want to confide in Rachael as a friend. The chaplain should also treat any information, such as the possibility that Queenie is drinking too much, with both caution and sensitivity at his next meeting with Queenie.

In a way, the situation of Tim nearly requires the chaplain to start all over again. Given the new information from Udi, the chaplain may have to *see* the situation anew, and realise that Tim's reaction of cowering has something to do with the chaplain's first appearance – many people who are not expecting a visit from the chaplain receive a shock if the chaplain appears prepared as if for the 'last rites' and the person may even think that the doctors have not been honest with them about their prognosis. One important thing when dealing with people with disabilities is not to make any assumptions, to be careful how we *judge*. It is all too easy to assume that a person does not understand or is not aware of events just because they are not able to communicate what they are thinking and feeling. It may take the chaplain some time to unravel what has led Tim to behave in the way that he is, and it may take even longer to gain Tim's trust. Udi may help here as Udi is Tim's key worker and presumably knows Tim well. There is a question of how and to what extent Tim's family should also be involved, especially if the chaplain thinks that the failure to tell Tim the truth about his mother's death is a major cause of Tim's distress. If Tim thinks that hospital is where his mother is, he may be trying to find her, hence his attempts to try and get out of the room.

Alternatively, Tim may be feeling distrustful of hospitals and hospital staff, if, as far as he is concerned, his mother has disappeared after a visit to the hospital. Although relatives may decide not to tell a person with disabilities about the death of a close family member for the best of reasons to avoid further distress, often the person with disabilities believes that their loved one has abandoned them because she no longer visits. In the long term, not telling someone can cause considerable problems. There are further issues to consider for people with, for instance, dementia, who ask repeatedly after a relative who has died and then seem to relive the 'news' each time they are reminded. Strategies like going through the day of the funeral or talking through what happened, even if it was some time ago, may help here. Telling someone that their loved one has 'gone away', or 'will be back soon', or even 'has gone to be with Jesus' may in fact cause confusion. Simple, plain language reinforced with assurance of support and care may be the best way forward. *Act* by assessing spiritual needs.

Prayer as the staple of all encounters with people is always also the first consideration. Chaplains are also well placed to organise annual memorial services or prayers for people who have suffered invisible bereavement. There is much consolation to be had in saying prayers with people who are bereaved and keeping their loved one in mind even long after their loved one's death if someone has not had the opportunity to mourn. **O**bservation is key, since many people are confused about their emotions or unable to express what they are feeling; it also acknowledges that there is a mix of feelings that both change and re-occur. Engaging with the bereaved person where they are enables the chaplain to validate feelings but also helps move people on so that they can be oriented towards the new realities of their situation. **T**ime is something that perhaps the chaplain can afford to give when other colleagues cannot. This is perhaps why many colleagues ask the chaplain to come with them to break bad news. **R**emembering the grief-stricken person in prayers and also in follow-up meetings is important because bereavement can be a lengthy process. Helping people to prepare funerals and think about practicalities can be a healing process and may give the bereaved person the opportunity to work through some of their grief. Inviting people to annual memorial services for miscarriage or stillbirth can be of particular help for those who feel that their grief is invisible or difficult to share with others. **Y**ou also must consider your own wellbeing.

Out of my depth and self-care

Knowing your strengths and limitations and knowing when to seek help are part of a chaplain's core competencies and simply good professional practice. Chaplains face many ethical issues and relationships of care that are frequently more complicated than they initially appear. Not only do chaplains have to know about practice, procedure and legal implications, they also have to be aware that they are opening up a space that is more often than not emotionally challenging. Making time for regular meetings with colleagues in the chaplaincy team and talking to people you trust while maintaining appropriate confidentiality can be lifelines. Proper supervision enables chaplains to reflect on their experiences and practice so that they can develop the skills of self-examination, empathy and healthy reflective self-criticism. Moreover, discussion with another chaplain practitioner gives added perspectives on situations.

Much of the chaplain's daily work involves dealing with grief and bereavement and to do this effectively the chaplain has to maintain something of a therapeutic distance while at the same time engaging with attentive and generous listening. This can only be done successfully with a grounding in prayer. Self-care is not a luxury nor is it a selfish act. Self-care is good stewardship, and you observe how you are and look after yourself, not only for yourself but also for the other people whose lives you touch. Reflecting on how you feel, what matters to you, what losses you face and how you face them are questions you ask of others, and so engage with these questions and ask them of yourself. Giving time to rest, proper nutrition and a good work–life balance are all the things that chaplains tend to prescribe for others and these apply equally to the chaplain. By remembering who you are as a chaplain and a faith representative you are more able to hold fast to what matters, to what you love, and to what is sacred. After all, as the saying goes, you cannot give what you do not have.

REFLECTION

How do you face your own losses?

Summary

Supporting people who are grief-stricken can be challenging, emotionally demanding and perhaps even overwhelming. Grief produces strong and complex feelings. It is important for chaplains to remember that they are there to listen and support, not to solve all problems. Through attentive listening, with acceptance, people often come to realise what they themselves must do, and part of the chaplain's role is to help a person work through this process. Rituals, sacraments and prayer services are valuable ways in which people can bear the tension caused by the complex emotions of grief and bereavement, following through time-tested community patterns of facing loss.

In healthcare, sometimes the chaplain is faced with competing loyalties, and personal integrity makes demands. Our last chapter explores some of the issues involved in conscience, conscientious objection and loyalty conflicts.

Chapter 11

CONSCIENTIOUS OBJECTION AND LOYALTIES

CASE STUDY

Veronica, a nurse, comes to the chaplain with a major concern. She has seen her colleague nurse Wendy giving out medication on the ward to elderly patients. Veronica knows that Wendy sometimes gets the medication wrong, and Veronica is usually on hand to correct her friend's mistakes. Each time Wendy has asked Veronica not to say anything, and Veronica has agreed so far. Veronica says that she does not want to get Wendy into trouble, but she is worried that there may be occasions when she is not at hand to help Wendy out. Meanwhile, the chaplain has concerns of his own. He has been told that some of the medical staff on the antenatal ward are pressuring women to have early terminations if their unborn babies are diagnosed with a risk of foetal abnormality. The chaplain also has a contract which specifies that he must conduct all funerals including those of aborted foetuses, and at times this involves discussions with the parents. Sometimes the funerals are of people who have no family or who have left their bodies to the hospital research team. The chaplain has been asked to conduct the funeral of someone who was definitely an adherent of a faith tradition that is not the chaplain's own.

> **REFLECTION**
>
> Who are you loyal to? How would you negotiate a conflict of loyalties?

Loyalties and identity

One aspect of ethical action concerns how we hold together who we are with what we do. A virtuous person acts with virtue, an ethical person would want to connect what they think, want, intend, and are, with what they do. To act outwardly with love and compassion yet at the same time with indifference or hate in the heart somehow tarnishes good acts. While ethics is about knowing the things that make demands on us such as legislation, guidelines and due processes, it goes beyond merely applying these to the case in hand. Some people might describe ethics as being true to yourself, acting with authenticity, and often this is explained in terms of acting according to your conscience.

Conscience is tied up with identity and loyalty. For some people, conscience is a voice that speaks in the heart, a voice urging a person to be consistent, to be true to their values and beliefs. This understanding of conscience can be understood by people of all faiths and none. Other people understand conscience as the voice of God speaking in their heart. Another way of looking at conscience is to see it as our considered judgement about whether a particular action is good or bad. This can be an action we are thinking of doing or an action we have already done. However, sometimes our conscience can get things wrong, and we make the wrong decision. To avoid mistakes we have to *see* what we are doing and *judge* what we want to do using practical wisdom; we have to know ourselves, be prepared to seek advice and be open to correction. It may be difficult to *act* if we think that we have limited knowledge or if we face the prospect of suffering or if the situation is perplexing, and in these cases we may need the courage to do the best we can and leave the rest to God.

If we think about the identity of a healthcare practitioner, we may link it to the capabilities and competencies of a professional. In this analysis of the healthcare practitioner's identity there is a horizontal dimension that leads the practitioner to their institution and to the people for whom they care. As a healthcare professional, the identity of the healthcare chaplain does also have this horizontal dimension. However, the chaplain has a more significant dimension, a vertical dimension, because the chaplain's vocation arises not simply from a desire to serve others but also from a call from God. Being a professional and even a volunteer in healthcare may involve personal motivation and a desire to do good, but it is something the person chooses and something the person can set aside. Following the vocation of a healthcare chaplain is responding to a calling, and therefore there is a loyalty to something beyond the chaplain – to the one who calls.

Identity lies at the heart of questions of loyalty. Central to the identity of, for instance, a Christian chaplain is belief in God's love and in the healing mission of Jesus. This faith gives rise to certain commitments that many people of different faiths and none can accept, such as respecting human dignity, cherishing life, promoting a holistic view of the human person, contributing to the common good, prioritising the needs of the marginalised, working for justice. However, these commitments stem from a particular attitude – that the person is responding to God by ministering to their fellow human beings.

Faith also gives voice to other commitments associated with specific theological and moral religious traditions. It may help to clarify identity that informs loyalties by seeing the chaplain as having three ways of being present: negotiated presence, pastoral presence and prophetic presence. The chaplain is seen as having a particular presence in the workplace. This is a negotiated presence, because the chaplain acts in an official capacity with all the responsibility that that entails as well as acting as an official representative of a particular faith tradition. At times, there are tensions between these two official capacities, because the chaplain is authorised by both and accountable to both, and they may make different demands. The chaplain has a pastoral presence because attentive listening and opening up a sacred space can transform situations and people. What is disclosed in that sacred space can lead to ethical dilemmas or a clash of loyalties. The chaplain has a prophetic presence because he is in a position to challenge prevailing dominant cultures, to bring injustice to light, to speak for those who have no voice or who are not listened to. This prophetic presence makes demands for the chaplain himself to proclaim.

However, a chaplain does not simply claim his identity, nor can he assume that his identity is readily understood by all. Where identity concerns a specific religious calling or vocation or role, this goes beyond personal identity, and it is validated by a particular community and a particular tradition. The healthcare chaplain belongs to a number of communities that inform his identity. The chaplain serves the healthcare community where people who are sick, suffering, vulnerable and in spiritual and existential need entrust their care to relative strangers. This community also comprises family, carers and close friends of patients, as well as other healthcare colleagues from students and porters, to volunteers and the healthcare organisation itself. Already, as we have seen in some of our case studies, there may be tensions in the relationships between all these members of this community. In this community, the chaplain is called to share the same ethical and moral standards as other healthcare professionals. However, beyond this network of relationships the chaplain is also placed in the wider human community from which he can understand questions of power, authority and responsibility related to his organisation. From this perspective, he advocates for the vulnerable and voiceless. The chaplain belongs to a disciplinary community, that is to say a professional body that holds the chaplain to standards of practice, knowledge, skill, competence, boundaries and professional development. Trust in chaplaincy is built on such disciplinary communities. However, the most defining characteristic of the identity of the chaplain is that he is a representative of a particular faith community, and this community transmits specific formation and theological training. A chaplain who, in partnership with a faith community, is appointed to a chaplaincy or spiritual care post as a representative of that faith community holds the authority of that faith community. In representing his faith community, the chaplain is in dialogue with the community he serves and with the professional community. At times, he may be a bridge between the different communities he serves.

In addition to possible tensions with the professional community, in many cases the chaplain will find that there is discrepancy between the practice of the faith community and the actual practice and beliefs of the person to whom he ministers, and this may cause further tensions. The chaplain is called to be sensitive to all these communities as he engages in practical pastoral and theologically informed care.

Information: conscientious objection and whistleblowing

Conscientious objection

Patients have a right to high-quality care that is clinically indicated and this care should be delivered in a supportive and non-judgemental way. At the same time, all healthcare practitioners and patients have personal beliefs and practices that are central to their lives and these need not be specifically religious beliefs. Article 9 of the Human Rights Act 1998 protects a person's right to freedom of thought, belief, conscience and religion. However, this is not an absolute right. A public authority can interfere with this right as long as the action of the authority is legal, necessary and proportionate and is to protect public order, health or morals, or the rights and freedoms of other people. There is some English legislation that refers specifically to the right to conscientious objection. For instance, under section 4(1) of the Abortion Act 1967, no one is under a duty to participate in any treatment authorised by the Act to which that person has a conscientious objection. This may protect medical staff who object to abortion from having to participate directly in terminations. However, it does not protect people who work at more of a distance, such as a secretary who writes up appointment letters. Nor does it protect midwives who, despite their previously stated objections to terminations, are asked to organise rotas for staff working on a ward where terminations are carried out.

The situation of a chaplain who has a conscientious objection to abortion but who is called to minister to a woman who is in the process of having a termination remains legally unclear. However, if a woman asks for a chaplain, the chaplain should seriously consider this so that he can ascertain precisely what support the woman has requested.

Sometimes it is useful to consider how to act in moral dilemmas in terms of cooperation. We cooperate in many common projects on a daily basis. However, the chaplain may be asked to be involved in what he considers to be someone else's wrong action. It would be wrong for the chaplain to act in a way that meant he shared in the person's wrongful aims – this is formal cooperation. However, if he helps but does not share those aims then his cooperation is material. Nevertheless, in many dilemmas the chaplain should perhaps witness to his prophetic presence and call attention to injustice or wrongdoing.

Many people argue that there must be a balance between the rights of patients and the freedom of practitioners to follow their sincerely held beliefs. Many hospital protocols state that healthcare staff may practise according to their beliefs as long as they follow the law, they do not treat patients unfairly, they do not deny access to appropriate medical treatment or services, and they do not cause patients distress. The law does allow practitioners to opt out of providing a particular procedure if it conflicts with personal beliefs and values, as long as this opting out does not result in discrimination or harassment against an individual patient or group of patients. Practitioners are advised to make patients aware of their conscientious objection in advance and to discuss with colleagues how they can practise in accordance with their beliefs without overburdening them and without compromising patient care. To a certain extent the very nature of a chaplain's religious affiliation makes this clear from the start. Any discussion of an objection to a procedure should not suggest judgement of a patient or their lifestyle and it should not cause distress. The practitioner should tell the patient that they can see another practitioner for treatment. A chaplain can help someone make a decision but the chaplain cannot make up that person's mind for them. Each one of us must learn to take responsibility for our own decisions and make those decisions as best we can.

Sharing concerns and whistleblowing

Sometimes things do go wrong with patient care, including issues from the perspective of chaplaincy, and it is crucial that mistakes are identified and reported early. Action should be taken to remedy the error if possible. It is good practice for an organisation to have a policy for reporting adverse incidents, and this should be followed. In addition, there is a professional duty to be open and honest when things go wrong – a duty of candour. An appropriate person such as the lead clinician should speak to the patient and an apology should be given.

Anyone who has a concern about the quality of patient care in a particular circumstance or situation should be able to make their concerns known to the appropriate person in their organisation and their concerns should be treated seriously, be assessed and, if necessary, be acted on. This is not only a matter of public accountability, transparency and due process, it is also a matter of trust. Healthcare professionals including chaplains have a duty to act if they think that a patient's safety is at risk or if the patient's care or dignity is being compromised. A person who raises a concern should not be blamed or suffer reprisals.

The object of sharing serious concerns is certainly related to patient safety. However, it is also related to good and bad practice, and so a significant part of sharing concerns is so that the organisation can reflect on and learn from bad practice. The point is for the organisation to see the message not the messenger. In order to be effective, the person bringing the concern to the attention of the organisation needs to be clear about the facts and details. The person should be fair in evaluating the situation without blame or exaggeration, and if possible, should suggest solutions. Following the procedures set out by the organisation, being helpful increases the opportunity for the organisation to learn from the concern. In terms of procedure, it is preferable to raise a concern at the earliest opportunity, usually first with a line manager or supervisor, so that the concern can be addressed before it becomes a more serious problem. If a person does not think that their concern has been adequately addressed they can escalate the concern internally at a more senior level. Although a person has the right to go directly to an appropriate external agency, it is sensible to seek advice from a professional body.

There are times when people have decided that their concerns have not been dealt with adequately enough by those in charge and that as a result patients are suffering. Whistleblowing happens when a person working in a particular organisation makes public certain acts, omissions, practices or policies that the person perceives to be morally wrong while the organisation itself sees that disclosure as being morally wrong. The concern must have a public interest aspect, usually because it compromises patient safety in some way, and in general it must be related to medical licensing, medical education, standards of medical professionalism and fitness to practice.

The Public Interest Disclosure Act 1998 came into force in 1999. Under the Act there is a right to raise a public concern but the whistleblower has to show this. Moreover, the legislation protects from dismissal only those who are in a working relationship with the organisation. A whistleblower can choose to remain anonymous but if they choose to give some personal details they can ask that these details are treated as confidential. However, if the body dealing with the concern thinks it necessary, details can be disclosed.

Disposal of foetal remains

How to deal with the remains of a foetus after pregnancy loss is a difficult issue, and on the whole there is no distinction made between losses that occur as a result of miscarriage and as a result of voluntary termination. Women who opt for a late-stage termination for foetal abnormality may not be fully aware of the procedure and may simply be told that the foetus is removed and dies as a result of the process. Since a live birth is considered to be an outcome that contradicts the intention of abortion, feticide is routinely carried out.

Under the Human Tissue Act 2004, 'pregnancy remains' are regarded as the tissue of the woman. Since the disposal of 'pregnancy remains' is a sensitive issue, generally the wishes of the woman concerned are paramount. However, there is a recognised minimum standard of options including burial, cremation and incineration. If the remains are incinerated, they are kept separate from clinical waste, yet at the same time the remains are treated as having no special status. It is good practice to give a woman information about the options and what might happen if she does not express an opinion. Regardless of the circumstances of the loss, hospitals should ensure that pregnancy remains are treated with respect, and the hospital is sensitive to the religious, spiritual and cultural practices of those involved. Records of how and when remains were disposed of should be kept.

Most people involved in the loss of a foetus have never had to arrange a funeral before. Some may arrange their own funeral, but many people leave the arrangements up to the hospital chaplain. Funerals do help to bring closure to a dark time in people's lives and for many people the experience of abortion is often accompanied by confusion, great pain and suffering. For some people, attempting to find forgiveness is a significant part of the process. The chaplain should be aware of the extent to which the funeral rites of his faith tradition can be adapted to the circumstances of the funeral liturgy for the baby and how prayers can be adapted to meet the needs of the family.

Case study: ethical implications

See: In some cases, by unravelling a situation and separating out its main elements the chaplain can help the person work out for themselves how to see the situation accurately. In cases where there is clear guideline or duties, these may help to clarify what should be done. Some people may argue that the outcome of a situation, for instance the respectful burial of the remains of babies, is the same whoever performs the relevant ritual. However, when thinking ethically we may wish to challenge those who think that only consequences matter. Religious rites are not merely a matter of outcomes, nor can they be demanded as if they are part of the consumer culture.

Judge: In the case of ministering to patients or of ritual prayers for people of a different faith tradition to yours as a chaplain, consider if you are really the person to carry out these acts.

Act: Remember to act with prayer and according to your properly formed and informed conscience. Keep a written account of your actions and expect timely feedback.

Some further comments

Under the guidelines of the General Medial Council a healthcare practitioner should *see* that she has the duty to raise concerns if she believes that patient safety or care is compromised. The chaplain should be aware of the protocol of the organisation for raising concerns and advise Veronica to follow it. The chaplain could also suggest that Veronica talks to Wendy in order to try and establish why she is making these mistakes. Veronica could then encourage Wendy to report the mistakes herself and to seek extra training as part of her continuing professional development. However, it seems as if Wendy expects Veronica to cover up for her and she is continuing to make what may amount to serious mistakes that jeopardise patient safety. Given that the situation is not changing and Veronica is already becoming complicit, Veronica should *judge* whether it is time to escalate the issue to the next level and speak to a senior colleague. After all, patient safety is at stake and this overrides colleague friendships. However, if Veronica decides to take no action, the chaplain is now in possession of knowledge that might compromise patient safety, and so he has the duty to raise his concerns. The chaplain must remember to make a record of the steps he has taken.

We saw in Chapter 6 that under the Abortion Act 1967 a termination may take place after 24 weeks only if the mother's life is in danger or if the foetus is at substantial risk of serious disability. We also noted that the terms 'substantial' and 'serious' have not been defined and some people argue that these terms are left to the subjective opinions of medical professionals. Moreover, some medical professionals may be of the opinion that a decision to terminate should be taken as soon as possible in order to prevent or at least lessen future psychological harm. Research shows that medical professionals do influence choices both in the way in which they present information and choices, and in what exactly they tell patients. However, patients are entitled to objective and non-judgemental medical advice and treatment regardless of a doctor's personal views; the doctor's right to act on their personal views is protected by conscientious objection.

The chaplain would do well to be clear on the information he has received so that he is sure of the facts. Gently reminding staff on the ward that good healthcare professionals work in partnership with patients, that they listen to patients and take account of their views, may be sufficient. However, in the situation of pressure put on vulnerable patients, the chaplain may find that he needs to be an advocate for the patient. If the chaplain still has serious concerns, then he should follow the protocol of the organisation by raising his concern with the appropriate person and escalating the concern if necessary. At times, the chaplain may be called on to be a prophet, to speak from the authority gained through his professional pastoral support of patients, families and colleagues. It is therefore important to keep a written account of your actions.

Helping individuals, families, carers and friends to mark the lives and deaths of their loved ones through ritual is a significant aspect of the chaplain's work. The ritual of a funeral helps to give meaning to a life lived, even if it was short. However, the funeral ritual is not merely a therapeutic exercise. Certainly, funerals can console those who are bereaved. However, in many faith traditions funerals celebrate the confident belief that death is not the end, nor does death break bonds with the living. The funeral service commends the deceased person, however small or young they may be, to the mercy of God. If we understand funeral services as not merely expressions of grief or sorrow but also as acts of worship and praise to a loving and merciful God, then the focus moves from the tragedy of what has happened. This is not to say that what happened is not significant and that is why prayers should reflect the needs of those present and the situation. There are many factors that influence a woman's decision to have a termination and such a decision can often be painful and shattering. While many faith traditions hold that abortion is a terrible wrong, faith traditions also acknowledge that a compassionate way forward is to accompany people so that they can come to understand what happened and to face it honestly. A funeral may be the first step on the path to healing the psychological wound of abortion and to forgiveness.

In many hospitals, the chaplaincy team operates in an ecumenical and multi-faith context. Chaplains are encouraged to work closely with colleagues of different Christian denominations and other faith traditions. As a matter of respect for a person's beliefs, if a person is of a particular faith then that person should be ministered to by a chaplain of their own tradition. Similarly, funeral rites and prayers are often distinctive of a particular faith tradition and so are appropriate for those who share in that tradition. Where practicable, a chaplain should attempt to find an appropriate minister to conduct the funeral of someone who is of a different faith tradition. As a matter of conscience, a chaplain should not be obliged to pray or conduct rites for which he has no authority nor should the chaplain pray to a deity that is not his own. However, the chaplain could offer to pray for the person within the chaplain's own faith tradition. In situations where the chaplain is praying for a person of a different faith tradition, he should be careful about the wording of prayers.

Pray, especially over hard decisions. **O**bserve to ensure you have discerned the facts and aspects relevant to your decisions. **E**ngage with the procedures and processes so that people can learn from what is happening and not simply feel as if they have attracted blame. Take **t**ime so that you are not rushed into hasty decisions. **R**emember who you are and what you stand for. Be true to **y**our conscience and to your faith tradition.

REFLECTION

What virtues are needed to be able to speak out about injustice?

Summary

To *see* asks the chaplain to journey alongside people in order to understand reality with the eyes of faith and heart of God. To *judge* asks the chaplain to look at the situation with theological reflection, and with mercy and compassion in the light of truth. To *act* calls the chaplain to draw on prayer, faith and hope in planning and carrying out what needs to be done or in working out the possible ways of 'being' in the new realities of the situation. To see, judge and act require the virtues of practical wisdom to be able to guide action; justice to respect human dignity; courage to pursue what should be done even if it costs; and a sense of balance in what we do.

As the prophet Micah says, 'And what does the Lord require of you? To *act* justly and to love mercy and to walk humbly with your God.'

Resources

Chaplaincy guidelines

NHS England Chaplaincy Guidelines (2015) *Promoting Excellence in Pastoral, Spiritual & Religious Care* – www.england.nhs.uk/wp-content/uploads/2015/03/nhs-chaplaincy-guidelines-2015.pdf

NHS Scotland (2009) *Spiritual Care and Chaplaincy* – www.ukbhc.org.uk/sites/default/files/Spiritual%20Care%20&%20Chaplaincy%20-%20NHS%20Scotland%20-%202009.pdf

NHS Wales (2010) *Standards for Spiritual Care in the NHS in Wales 2010 Supporting Guidance* – www.ukbhc.org.uk/sites/default/files/Spiritual%20Care%20Supporting%20Guidance%20-%20NHS%20in%20Wales%202010.pdf

Chaplaincy code of conduct and standards

UK Board of Healthcare Chaplaincy (2006) *Standards for Hospice and Palliative Care Chaplaincy* – www.ukbhc.org.uk/sites/default/files/ahpcc_standards_for_hospice_and_palliative_care_chaplaincy_2006.pdf

UK Board of Healthcare Chaplaincy (2007) *Standards for NHS Scotland Chaplaincy Services 2007* – www.ukbhc.org.uk/sites/default/files/standards_for_nhsscotland_chaplaincy_service_2007.pdf

UK Board of Healthcare Chaplaincy (2009) *Standards for Healthcare Chaplaincy Services 2009* – www.ukbhc.org.uk/sites/default/files/standards_for_healthcare_chapalincy_services_2009.pdf

UK Board of Healthcare Chaplaincy (2010, revised 2014) *Code of Conduct for Healthcare Chaplains* – www.ukbhc.org.uk/sites/default/files/ukbhc_code_of_conduct_2010_revised_2014_0.pdf

Person-centred care

Dementia Friends – www.dementiafriends.org.uk

Department of Health (2015) *The NHS Constitution for England* – www.gov.
uk/government/uploads/system/uploads/attachment_data/file/480482/
NHS_Constitution_WEB.pdf

Department of Health, Social Services and Public Safety (2017) *Quality 2020:
A Ten-year Strategy to Protect and Improve Quality in Health and Social
Care in Northern Ireland* – www.health-ni.gov.uk/publications/quality-
2020-ten-year-strategy-protect-and-improve-quality-health-and-social-
care

Health and Social Care Act 2012 – www.legislation.gov.uk/ukpga/2012/7/
contents/enacted

NHS Scotland (2013) *Everyone Matters: 2020 Workforce Vision* – www.gov.
scot/Resource/0042/00424225.pdf

Scottish Government (2012) *Charter of Patient Rights and Responsibilities* –
www.gov.scot/Resource/0039/00390989.pdf

Welsh Government (2015) *Health and Care Standards* – www.wales.
nhs.uk/sitesplus/documents/1064/24729_Health%20Standards%20
Framework_2015_E1.pdf

Williams, A. *The Listening Organisation: Ensuring Care is Person-Centred in
NHS Wales.* Cardiff: 1000 Lives Plus – www.1000livesplus.wales.nhs.uk/
sitesplus/documents/1011/1000%20Lives%20Plus%20-%20%27The%20
Listening%20Organisation%27%20white%20paper%20WEB.pdf

Capabilities and competencies

NHS Education for Scotland (2008) *Spiritual and Religious Care Capabilities
and Competences for Healthcare Chaplains* – www.ukbhc.org.uk/sites/
default/files/nes_chaplaincy_capabilities_and_competencies.pdf

NHS Wales (2010) *Guidance on Capabilities and Competences for Healthcare
Chaplains/Spiritual Care Givers in Wales 2010* – www.ukbhc.org.uk/
sites/default/files/Spiritual%20%26%20Religious%20Capabilities%20
%26%20Competences%20-%20NHS%20in%20Wales.pdf

UK Board of Healthcare Chaplaincy (2017) *Spiritual and Religious Care
Capabilities and Competences for Healthcare Chaplains Bands 5, 6, 7 and 8*
– www.ukbhc.org.uk/sites/default/files/ukbhc_spiritual_and_religious_
capabilities_and_competences_bands_5_-_8_2017.pdf

Confidentiality

Department of Health (2003) *Confidentiality: NHS Code of Practice, November 2003* – https://assets.publishing.service/gov.uk/government/uploads/system/uploads/attachment_data/file/200146/Confidentiality_-_NHS_Code_of_Practice.pdf

Department of Health (2010) *Confidentiality: NHS Code of Practice, Supplementary Guidance: Public Interest Disclosure, November 2010* – www.gov.uk/government/uploads/system/uploads/attachment_data/file/216476/dh_122031.pdf

Safeguarding

NHS England Safeguarding Policy 2015

Department for Education (2015) *Working Together to Safeguard Children: A Guide to Inter-agency Working to Safeguard and Promote the Welfare of Children March 2015* – www.gov.uk/government/uploads/system/uploads/attachment_data/file/592101/Working_Together_to_Safeguard_Children_20170213.pdf

Department for Education (2015) *What To Do if You Are Worried a Child is Being Abused: Advice for Practitioners* – www.gov.uk/government/uploads/system/uploads/attachment_data/file/419604/What_to_do_if_you_re_worried_a_child_is_being_abused.pdf

General Medical Council (2017) *GMC Guidance on Whistleblowing* – www.gmc-uk.org/DC5900_Whistleblowing_guidance.pdf_57107304.pdf

End-of-life care

Leadership Alliance for the Care of Dying People (2014) *One Chance to Get it Right* – www.gov.uk/government/uploads/system/uploads/attachment_data/file/323188/One_chance_to_get_it_right.pdf

The Art of Dying Well – www.artofdyingwell.org

The Catholic Bishops' Conference of England & Wales (2010) *A Practical Guide to the Spiritual Care of the Dying Person* – www.cbcew.org.uk/content/download/34854/.../spiritual-care-of-dying-2010.pdf

Further reading

Ash, A. (2016) *Whistleblowing and Ethics in Health and Social Care*. London: Jessica Kingsley Publishers.

Brown, M. (2011) *Tensions in Christian Ethics: An Introduction*. London: SPCK (Society for Promoting Christian Knowledge).

Catholic Bishops of England and Wales (2004) *Cherishing Life*. London: The Catholic Truth Society.

Graham, M. and Cowley, J. (2015) *A Practical Guide to the Mental Capacity Act 2005*. London: Jessica Kingsley Publishers.

Gula, R. (2010) *Just Ministry*. New York, NY: Paulist Press.

Hilsman, G. (2016) *Spiritual Care in Common Terms: How Chaplains Can Effectively Describe the Spiritual Needs of Patients in Medical Records*. London: Jessica Kingsley Publishers.

McCoy, A. (2004) *An Intelligent Person's Guide to Christian Ethics*. London: Continuum.

Misselbrook, D. (2001) *Thinking About Patients*. Oxford: Radcliffe Publishing.

Neuberger, J. (2004) *Caring for Dying People of Different Faiths*. Abingdon: Radcliffe Medical Press.

Pye, J., Sedgwick, P. and Todd, A. (eds) (2015) *Critical Care: Delivering Spiritual Care in Healthcare Contexts*. London: Jessica Kingsley Publishers.

Robinson, S. (2008) *Spirituality, Ethics and Care*. London: Jessica Kingsley Publishers.

Vardy, P. (2012) *Ethics Matters*. London: SCM Press.

Index